The Shakespearean Metaphor

Studies in Language and Form

Ralph Berry

Routledge
Taylor & Francis Group

First published in 1978
by The MacMillan Press Ltd

This edition first published in 2017 by Routledge
2 Park Square, Milton Park, Abingdon, Oxon, OX14 4RN
and by Routledge
711 Third Avenue, New York, NY 10017

Routledge is an imprint of the Taylor & Francis Group, an informa business

Publisher's Note
The publisher has gone to great lengths to ensure the quality of this reprint but points out that some imperfections in the original copies may be apparent.

Disclaimer
The publisher has made every effort to trace copyright holders and welcomes correspondence from those they have been unable to contact.

A Library of Congress record exists under LC control number: 78318058

ISBN 13: 978-1-138-22168-0 (hbk)
ISBN 13: 978-1-315-40949-8 (ebk)
ISBN 13: 978-1-138-22178-9 (pbk)

THE SHAKESPEAREAN METAPHOR

Studies in Language and Form

Ralph Berry
Professor of English
York University, Ontario

First published 1978 by
THE MACMILLAN PRESS LTD
London and Basingstoke
Associated companies in Delhi
Dublin Hong Kong Johannesburg Lagos
Melbourne New York Singapore Tokyo

Printed in Great Britain by
THE BOWERING PRESS LTD
Plymouth

British Library Cataloguing in Publication Data

Berry, Ralph
The Shakespearean metaphor
1. Shakespeare, William—Criticism and interpretation 2. Metaphor
I. Title
822.3'3 PR2997.M/
ISBN 0-333-23176-7

TO MY FATHER AND MOTHER

Contents

Acknowledgements

The chapter on *Hamlet* first appeared in *Shakespeare Survey 28* (1975). That on *Coriolanus* was originally published (in a slightly different form) in *Studies in English Literature 1500–1900* (1973), to whose Editor I am indebted for permission to reprint. I wish also to thank the University of Manitoba, for a grant towards secretarial assistance in the preparation of this book.

R.B.

Introduction

This book is a study of some ways in which Shakespeare exploits the possibilities of metaphor. Clearly, the terrain is too vast to permit of general or definitive coverage; and I present, therefore, a series of case-histories, from the early and mature Shakespeare. The play itself is in each case the sole area of investigation. My prime interest is in metaphor as a controlling structure, and my aim in each play is to detect the extent to which a certain metaphoric idea informs and organises the drama.

The 'controlling metaphor' is a way of identifying the dramatic object which it is the critic's business to describe. It is perhaps most easily visible in some of the early plays. In *King John* the bastardy/legitimacy idea is energised by the major acting part. There is a kind of formal priority here to the metaphor I describe. Similarly, the Chorus/Sonnet of *Romeo and Juliet* and the Chorus/Authorised Version of *Henry V* make their own claims for special consideration. But generally, exclusive priority cannot be claimed for a metaphoric formation. That is because different metaphoric ideas co-exist easily within the same play. Metaphors do not eject each other in the way that physical entities do: it is perfectly possible to see *Richard III* as founded on the idea of the play, or to pursue the implications of the tree/garden/seasonal imagery. And the mature Shakespeare finds ways of building more and more patterns of approximately equal status into his dramatic structures. So one can scarcely hope to identify more than a major organising principle. The play is always subject to other formulations.

Still, to select a metaphoric formation is always a critical act of some promise. One holds the play up to the light, and views it via that single angle of incidence. To see *Troilus and Cressida*, say, as stemming from the association that Ovid phrases as 'tempus edax rerum' is to account for much within that marvellous structure. I argue, simply, for a sustained act of perception from a single angle, for the description that allows me best to account for the drama.

In these matters the relation of metaphor to symbol is a recurring issue. In the most general sense, we can postulate a common origin to metaphor and symbol : perception of association. But the two seem to work in opposed directions. A symbol generates associations, while a metaphor grasps towards analogy. There is an element of passivity about the perception of symbol, whereas metaphor is an active attempt to grapple with reality. Metaphors are, or should be, striking. Symbols are, or should be, satisfying and inevitable. Metaphors are irritable, appetent : they seek an ever-elusive fruition, a state of definition. Symbols imply content, an acceptance of a provisional codification of reality. They rest on the awareness of meanings that are reflected back from the object. Thus, Marvell's 'Upon Appleton House' is based on a sequence of symbolic perceptions :

> And see how Chance's better Wit
> Could with a Mask my studies hit!
> (LXXIV)

These include the recognition of the Mowers as the adversaries in the Civil Wars, and the flooded field as a type of chaos. Similarly, the old Churchill, gazing into a log fire : 'I know what it's like to be a log : reluctant to be consumed but yielding in the end to persuasion.'[1] These distinctions are convenient for discourse; but a Shakespeare play is constantly casting doubt on their absolute utility. Let me cite a few instances. The banished Duke in *As You Like It* finds 'sermons in stones', that is, reads symbolic values into his immediate environment. These values are transferred directly into terms that we conventionally regard as metaphors. 'The poor dappled fools, / Being native burghers of the desert city' is the Duke's account of the deer. Jacques independently perceives the same association and elaborates it into a string of conceits : 'Sweep on, you fat and greasy citizens; / 'Tis just the fashion : wherefore do you look / Upon that poor and broken bankrupt there?' The play hereabouts presents the Forest as a symbol of human society, and the individual metaphors take up the idea in verbally striking form. Again, Polixenes' address to Perdita poses the same problem :

> You see, sweet maid, we marry
> A gentler scion to the wildest stock,
> And make conceive a bark of baser kind
> By bud of nobler race : this is an art
> Which does mend nature, change it rather, but
> The art itself is nature.
> (*The Winter's Tale*, IV, 4, 92–7)

Polixenes believes himself to be using a metaphor : the human term of 'gentler scion' is applied to a plant. But his own son, the 'gentler scion' Florizel, is wooing the shepherdess Perdita. The metaphor therefore picks up an actuality of the drama. Moreover, the play poses a larger question: if 'gentler scion' is a metaphor for a plant, may not a plant be a metaphor for human life? The axes of *The Winter's Tale* are spring/winter, youth/age, birth/rebirth: flowers and humanity have essentially equal status in the drama. I think, then, that strict metaphor/symbol distinctions are helpful in purely local contexts only. Overall, in the total play, one employs a different mode of judgment. Here the collective force of associative patterns (established by recurrence) is everything. A symbol may be perceived by an individual in a play, passively. A group of such symbols does not simply happen to congregate in a play. Plays are not written passively. One needs a means of identifying the associations that are projected: and 'metaphor' I use not only for a local grasping after associative likeness, but the playwright's central impulse in bringing together numerous perceptions of association to organise and express a dramatic action.

It would be convenient to assert that with 'metaphor' one could confine oneself to figurative language. But one cannot safely do so. It follows naturally from the difficulties of distinguishing between symbol and metaphor that there is a similarly blurred frontier between literal and figurative. A symbol will often be a literal fact, and referred to locally in non-figurative language. When Henry VI says 'Yea, man and birds are fain of climbing high' he is stating a fact that springs directly from his observation of the falcon-hunt. It is nonetheless a perception of association. One has to be on one's guard against assuming an absolute divergence between literal and figurative in Shakespeare. Formal comparisons aside, let us take a single instance, Ulysses' 'No trumpet answers' (*Troilus and Cressida*, IV, 5, 11). By all conventional standards, this is unarguably a literal statement of a literal fact. But the three words are the play. The chivalric trumpet has sounded and silence, heavy, deflating, mocking descends. A gesture founded on a certain value-system has been made, and receives a negative answer. The silence that follows the trumpet invests with a special weight the meaning of the situation, and in breaking the silence Ulysses interprets it, states it, realises it. It is an easy judgement, then, to say that the trumpet (together with the style of Ajax's admonition to the trumpeter) and the subsequent silence symbolise the play; for the total action does indeed accord with this single moment of inflation and deflation.[2] But once we speak of a single event 'symbolising', or 'representing' the play, we are examining the foundations of literal language (in a poetic, completely unified drama, that is). So one is forced back upon the position that *all* the language of a Shakespeare play is a vehicle to express meaning: and the customary distinctions between figurative and literal statements merely locate what one notices most easily, the rocks thrusting up from the surfaces of language. They are not, however, in all cases the most reliable of guides to contours of the land. And this explains the variable quality of so many image-studies, beginning with Caroline Spurgeon's classic *Shakespeare's Imagery.* With certain plays, an image analysis immediately picks up vital concerns. I instance the picture/idol images in *The Two Gentlemen of Verona,* the clothing images in *Macbeth,* the food images in *Troilus and Cressida.* In other plays (say, *Much Ado About Nothing*), the method fails. It assumes a readily detectable, formal distinction between metaphoric and non-metaphoric that does not correspond to the realities of the drama. The positive results of an image investigation are often striking and valid, the negative conclusions very dubious. The critic's imperative, then, is to maintain a sense of the multitude of relations between literal and figurative language, and to keep his categories fluid and provisional. It is important to detect the accumulation of 'right' in *King John,* to perceive the drift of the sexual metaphors energised by the Bastard, and to make the necessary connections. In talking about 'metaphor' one is committed, simply, to talking about as much 'literal' language as one needs.

Could we proceed a long step further, and abandon as useless to our purposes all category-distinctions that separate literal from metaphoric, at least in the context of poetic drama? That would be supremely rash. A. D. Nuttall makes the point neatly:

> . . . the claim that all discourse is metaphorical, if granted, does not destroy my thesis only. It also destroys itself. To say that all discourse is metaphorical is to empty the word 'metaphorical' of all content. The concept 'metaphorical', in fact, presupposes the concept 'literal'. We say that a word is metaphorical when we perceive that it has been transferred from its proper, literal, application. If we claim that there is no such thing as a 'proper, literal, application', we shall find it hard to explain how people ever arrived at the conception of a 'transferred term'. The concept 'borrow' has no meaning for the man who lacks the concept of property. We may assert, if we wish, that 'style' is a metaphor drawn from a physical object, a pen, but we make the modern term metaphorical only by allowing a literal sense to its etymological ancestor. If 'pen' was never the literal meaning of 'style', then the modern use can scarcely be described as a metaphor drawn from the world of physical objects. If 'pen' is no more the literal meaning of 'style' than is 'manner of writing', then it is impossible to say that one is a metaphor from the other. We

are left with a mere series of meanings, which is not at all the same thing as a series of metaphors.[3]

There is a fundamental philosophic problem in admitting 'metaphoric' save in relation to 'literal'; but more than that, Shakespeare has an exceptional sense of the dynamic relations between the two, hence of the impress of language upon the human mind. Everyone is familiar with the idea that a single word may express multiple possibilities. So indeed it may, but at the heart of this is Shakespeare's sense of the ineradicable dualism of language, the reciprocity of metaphor and literal. To state the matter crudely (but, I think, necessarily): Shakespeare's language advances two propositions: 'This is *like*', and 'this *is*'. The first proposition is that of metaphor and figurative, the second that of symbol and literal. Neither statement exists independently of the other. We consider each statement in relation to the other, within a single context: the play.

Even within the local context, this dualism is readily perceived. Take Buckingham's 'Had you not come upon your cue, my lord, / William Lord Hastings had pronounc'd your part' (*Richard III*, III, 4, 27–8). 'Cue' might be a dead or moribund metaphor, meaning no more than 'signal' and thus close to literal; 'part', similarly, is sufficiently camouflaged as literal to merge with its landscape. But of course we assume Buckingham's ironic awareness of the implications. 'Cue-part' is then more than a trope, a mere witticism; it may express the psychological reality (for both Buckingham and Richard) that they are acting as on a stage. We need both possibilities, not because one or other has to be selected but because the mental reality (for the speaker, and for us) is a state that grasps both possibilities. But how can we characterise this state? We might conceive of Buckingham's mind here as maintaining an equilibrium consisting of oscillation between the two major possibilities, 'this is *like*' and 'this *is*'. As a more advanced example, take Prospero's 'Our revels now are ended' speech. The core of this is association between mortality and the stage. But which part is mortality, which the theatre? As I argue later (pp. 112–13) the syntax of this passage defies a consistent reading. Every time we accept one provisionally, the major alternative displaces it. As with syntax, so with the core metaphor: the formal difficulty of reading the passage destroys our sense of the conventional tenor-vehicle distinction. The mind shifts from one frame to the other, from 'globe' (earth) to 'Globe' (theatre). The mental process resembles that of a trick drawing in which we move from one interpretation to another.[4]

These instances are small-scale models of what the total play may do to us. The overall experience can be that of a shift from our sense of the literal to the metaphoric. Thus in *The Merchant of Venice*, 'venture' starts out as a purely commercial undertaking, with a restricted technical sense, and mutates (via Portia's 'Before you venture for me') into a figure for human gain.[5] The blindness-seeing imagery in *King Lear*, together with the actualities of the drama, form a central vehicle for knowledge. In *Antony and Cleopatra*, 'Egypt-Rome' becomes a way of coding two complexes of values. Geographic location supplies a referent of values, in addition to identifying the simplest of physical facts. The essence of the matter is repetition and recall: a word retained in a new context receives new meanings, and retroactively affects the old. I emphasise that a multiplicity of possibilities emerges from these complex phenomena: but I put it, that Shakespeare's principle of organisation permits him always to relate these possibilities to the central dualism of metaphor and literal.

The studies here turn constantly to the relations between literal and metaphoric. *Player* is the metaphor for self in *Richard III*, and it becomes an organising principle, the play's two movements being the actor's immersion in role-playing and confrontation with reality. In *King John* the controlling metaphor for the issues of right and authority is bastardy and legitimacy, and the metaphor is incarnate in Faulconbridge. These early plays advance relatively direct, schematic ways of using a central metaphor to order the drama. Thereafter Shakespeare evolves subtler, more diffuse strategies. I regard both *Romeo and Juliet* and *Henry V* as being dominated by the idea of the Chorus. The Chorus in *Romeo and Juliet*, the incarnation of the sonnet, introduces a play whose inhabitants cannot break out of the mental limitations of the sonnet. They live, speak, and die in a sonnet world. Here, the Chorus is the play, or at least the society of the play. In *Henry V* the Chorus is the spokesman of the Official Version of the campaign, which the main events of the play do not precisely corroborate. He is an emblem of public rhetoric that is not entirely self-justifying. This central discrepancy between Chorus and play is coded in the succession of 'therefores', the collective hinge to the play's dubious logic.

Hamlet will not yield to any simple schema, and the prime metaphors of the play – corruption and death, acting, fighting – have often been analysed. I propose a term that is strictly not metaphoric at all, but which Shakespeare uses as the binding agent: *one*. 'To say one. . .' is Hamlet's understanding of the equipoise between self and situation, the moment when metaphor becomes actuality. The uppermost metaphor in Hamlet's mind, from the beginning of Act Five, Scene Two on, is that of the duellist. Hence the final passages are a realisation of the self as duellist; and of the self in other metaphoric formulations. Hamlet is fated to enact his own metaphors.

The two following studies revert to a more conventional treatment of image formations. *Troilus and Cressida* is well known for its accumulation of food images, but it is their connection with Time that I stress here. The sexual images in *Coriolanus* (read in conjunction with the images of acting) supply an interpretation of the entire play, but most especially a verdict on its hero. These images too must be related to certain non-metaphoric references to sexual congress.

The Tempest is the hardest of Shakespeare's plays to think about. It is nonetheless the conclusion to his work, and in effect as near to a conclusion as this book can arrive at. Any schema that one offers will look especially crass, a cave drawing of an exceptionally complex object. I suggest that we think of the play's dramatic essence as the experience of half-perceiving, half-grasping for truth. The relationship between metaphor and symbol is in fact the experience of *The Tempest*, with its progression of half-heard sounds, half-glimpsed vistas, half-understood correspondences. The play comes to us, and as we reach out for its meaning it eludes us. In dialectical terms, we can think of the play as a constant alternation between vision and reality. And this alternation touches on all the metaphoric motifs that occur in the play. I have analysed *The Tempest* in terms of power and possession, since this appears to me the dominant metaphoric motif. It leads up to the definition of self in terms of possession and surrender, and the point at which Shakespeare stops the play is our final clue to the priority of issues and motifs. The last word in the canon, for most of us, is 'free' : and the word's status remains equivocal and provisional. *Free* is the final instance of the recurring tension in Shakespeare between metaphor and actuality. It is perhaps the pulse of his drama.

1 *Richard III*: Player and King

A major organising metaphor for *Richard III* is the actor, together with play/audience. Obviously, the actor metaphor covers the manœuvrings of the central figure. More than that, it structures the play. *Richard III* has two movements, the caesura occurring at Richard's achievement of the crown; it is thus entirely satisfactory to account for the play, as does A. P. Rossiter, as a two-part structure of irony, 'the basic pattern of retributive justice.'[1] I want here to relate this account to the actor concept: the first half of *Richard III* describes an actor immersed in role-playing, the second half shows him confronting the realities from which his playing had excluded him.

I

Since 'actor' contains a built-in trap, we should begin with it. It must not be confused with dissimulation. Dissimulation is merely the necessary consequence of executing certain parts. The shifts and devices of Richard are the public manifestation, even a vulgarisation, if you like, of his role-playing. To 'act' is to perform before an audience, but not to deceive it, and not – though here we stir the depths of the actor's mind – oneself. The earliest refutation of the idea that Richard is an 'actor' because he is a deceiver is supplied by Henry VI. Alone of his society, he penetrates Richard's identity with this : 'What scene of death hath Roscius now to act?' (*3 Henry VI*, v, 6, 10). There is no question of Richard deceiving anyone at this point (save himself). But the gap between self and role opens out even here, in the logical inadequacy of his meditation :

> O, may such purple tears be always shed
> From those that wish the downfall of our house !
> .... I have no brother, I am like no brother ...
>
> (v, 6, 64–5, 80)

He kills Henry as an enemy to his house; he denies that the house, as a mental reality, exists. It will not do; the whole soliloquy is an extended self-exculpation, clear enough in

> And so I was; which plainly signified
> That I should snarl and bite and *play the dog*.
> Then, since the heavens have shaped my body so,
> Let hell make crook'd my mind to answer it.
> (v, 6, 76–9)

In blaming heaven, he acknowledges it. No further proof is needed of the logical imbecility of his argument. The role of playing the dog is not imposed on him by Providence, it is merely a reaction to the deficiencies of his physical heritage. And the 'glorious crown' of the great Act III soliloquy in *3 Henry VI* indicates the role that, of all others, he longs to play; because it 'round impales' (i.e. protects) his 'mis-shaped trunk'.

The situation has become stabilised by the opening of *Richard III*. Richard is at some distance from the psychic pain of *3 Henry VI*; having come to terms with himself, he announces his conclusion as an apparently logical inference, and as an act of will: 'And therefore, since I cannot prove a lover . . . / I am determined to prove a villain' (I, 1, 28–30). The interesting feature here is the technical nature of the soliloquy. Nicholas Brooke characterises it thus: 'this is not, however, soliloquy in the sense of the speaker talking to himself: it is an address to the audience, not so much taking them into his confidence as describing himself.'[2] The distinction is useful, but I think we can have it both ways. Richard, in thinking his thoughts aloud, addresses himself to a mental audience: that audience is *there*, in his imagination. I take it for granted that the actor, at this point, will always speak directly to the audience – the physical reality of the theatre is the incarnation of the psychological.[3] It is an extraordinary fusion of the Vice's direct address, and the perception that Richard needs an audience.

The rhetoric of the opening soliloquy seems exaggerated, affected, and removed some distance from the ironically disdainful consciousness of the speaker.[4] For the understanding of Richard's sensibility here, we can draw on the concept of 'camp'. The word has had some currency of recent years as a way of identifying a certain mode of behaviour. I use the term not in its sense of 'kitsch' – that is, displaying a banal and mediocre artistic quality – but in the sense supplied by the A-G Supplement to the *OED* (1972): 'ostentatious, exaggerated, affected, theatrical.' Those are the premier senses: the additional possibilities of 'homosexual' are not obviously relevant here. The classic description of the mode is Susan Sontag's, in her 'Notes on Camp', and some of her observations do help us to come closer to Richard's mind. 'Camp is a certain mode of aestheticism. It is one way of seeing the world as an aesthetic phenomenon.'[5] Camp has clear affinities with the theatre: Sontag refers to it on several occasions as 'the theatricalization of experience',[6] viewing it as 'the farthest extension, in sensibility, of the metaphor of life as theater.'[7] Let us regard camp, then, as a mannered projection of self that reflects an intense appreciation of being-as-role-playing. Now Richard, evidently, is seized with the delights of the actor's address to the world. He takes it well beyond an exploitation of the actor's craft as a political means to a political end. And this is apparent in the extravagance and panache with which each *part*, within the central mode of *actor*, is pursued. M. C. Bradbrook has detailed several: '. . . among the many parts in his wardrobe, that of the Plain Blunt Man is his favourite. With Clarence he plays the Honest Soldier, with Anne the Lovesick Hero.'[8] Later he becomes the 'Pious Contemplative'. Richard's role-playing has a farouche, inverted-comma quality; particularly is this true of the wooing-scene, in which Richard appears to be calling across time to the yet unborn spirit of Colley Cibber. It is pure Drama of Sensibility; and Miss Bradbrook's capitals are precisely what we need, to understand Richard throughout these activities.

The language of Richard tends to express this quality I seek to isolate. It is mannered, prone to certain stylistic shifts, very much aware of itself. Consider the heavily adjectival nature of the opening soliloquy. In the first twenty lines there are as many adjectives: 'stern alarums', 'merry meeting', 'amorous looking-glass', 'wanton ambling nymph'. The adjectives interpose a mental buffer between self and others; through adjectives one controls objects and people. It's a form of naming. Here, one catches that quality of seeing everything in inverted commas that Sontag discerns as a mark of camp.[9] A woman ceases to be a woman – she becomes a 'woman', or 'nymph', or even 'Nymph'. (The typographic conventions of our own age can help bring out the innate qualities of Shakespeare's words.) Then, there is the equally mannered bluntness of the Plain Man mode. John Palmer identifies the 'vernacular quality of Richard's speech. It is one of his favourite tricks.'[10] Thus, there is the taste for proverbial expressions: 'But yet I run before my horse to market' (I, 1, 166): 'Small herbs have grace, great weeds do grow apace' (II, 4, 13): 'So wise so young, they say, do never live long' (III, 1, 79): 'Short summers lightly have a forward spring' (III, 1, 94). It is, perhaps, a perception of self in a mock pastoral – Colin Clout among the courtiers. Sometimes the transition from trope to bluntness is the effect that Richard seems to relish: 'Your eyes drop millstones, when fools' eyes drop tears: / I like you, lads; about your business straight' (I, 3, 354–5). Here Richard becomes the Actor-

Manager, sending some stage hands about their business. Or, in a reverse transition, Buckingham's plea – the language is the spare mode of total political realism – encounters a mocking, distancing rhetoric that further gilds and protects the self, before yielding to simple statement:

Buckingham My lord, whoever journeys to the prince,
For God's sake, let not us two be behind;
For, by the way, I'll sort occasion,
As index to the story we late talked of,
To part the queen's proud kindred from the king.
Gloucester My other self, my counsel's consistory,
My oracle, my prophet! My dear cousin,
I, like a child, will go by thy direction.
Towards Ludlow then, for we'll not stay behind.
(II, 2, 146–54)

Here, I think, we detect the Star graciously accepting a minor role in a tactical operation – and, naturally, stealing the scene. The transitions, with Richard, are very considerably the essence of his appreciation of style.

The consequence, and therefore the objective of this immersion in role-playing is clear: Richard insulates himself against a central reality, the existence of a moral order. If the world is an aesthetic phenomenon, the categories of good and evil dissolve; thus Richard is not a villain, but a person playing a villain. The actor, as actor, sheds responsibility for the actions committed in the name of the role. He retreats from moral responsibility to technical expertise, to aesthetic excellence. For the Richard of the first half, experience becomes 'a victory of "style" over "content", "aesthetics" over "morality", of irony over tragedy.'[11] It is precisely the affair of the second half to reverse this multiple victory, to demonstrate that life, as Sontag observes, is not stylish.

II

All this leads us directly to the central verb of Richard's existence, *play*. He uses it himself on three occasions only, but it defines his mode of existence, and with it the entire play:

And seem a saint, when most I play the devil.
(I, 3, 338)

> O Buckingham, now do I play the touch,
> To try if thou be current gold indeed.
> (IV, 2, 8–9)
>
> Under our tents I'll play the eavesdropper,
> To see if any mean to shrink from me.
> (V, 3, 221–2)

These passages (to which can be added Buckingham's advice, 'Play the maid's part, still answer nay, and take it', III, 7, 51) are the story of the play: delight, test, fear. Now, the quantity of linguistic and psychological information coded in 'play' is staggering, as may be judged from the briefest of glances at the *OED*'s thirty-six senses. But we have at least to note the major implications of 'play' in addition to the uppermost sense here, 'to perform dramatically'. The *OED* supplies six main heads. 'I: To exercise oneself, act or move energetically; II: To exercise oneself in the way of diversion or amusement; III: To engage in a game; IV: To exercise oneself or engage in sword-play, fighting, or fencing; V: To perform instrumental music; VI: To perform dramatically.' Only V appears to me an unwanted sense,[12] in the larger context of Richard's activities. All the others are subsumed in, and are dramatised by, 'play' as projected in *Richard III*. We are, I suggest, in the realm of *homo ludens*. Johan Huizinga, in his study of man at play, gives the lead here: he argues for a broad, inclusive understanding of 'play'. After a survey of the word's origin (Old English plega, plegan), together with the corresponding terms in Old Saxon, Old High German, and Old Frisian, he concludes:

> Who can deny that in all these concepts – challenge, danger, contest, etc. – we are very close to the play-sphere? Play and danger, risk, chance, feat – it is all a single field of action where something is at stake.[13]

All this applies fairly obviously to Richard; one need not argue it at length. Activity, challenge, contest are his life.[14] 'Bustle', for instance, is his verb too: 'And leave the world for me to bustle in' (I, 1, 152): 'Come, bustle, bustle; caparison my horse' (V, 3, 289). Again, the idea of bodily movement in play may well be present in 'O Buckingham, now do I play the touch, / To try if thou be current gold indeed.' Curiously, Huizinga quotes this passage[15] as a casual illustration of the wider significance of 'play' in later English. I should regard it as a strategic ambiguity. The uppermost sense of 'play' here is surely what modern editions customarily give, 'to act the part of the touchstone': the phrase parallels the other instances of 'play' in *Richard III*. Still, the phrase could reasonably be taken to mean 'apply the touchstone', or even 'play the touchstone' (move a piece, as in a game). The 'game' sense does link up with a sector of the play sphere, of central importance to Richard, and this requires some demonstration. As early as *3 Henry VI*, Richard's taunting card-image signals a train of clues to his cast of mind:

> Alas, that Warwick had no more forecast,
> But whiles he thought to steal the single ten,
> The king was slily finger'd from the deck!
> (v, 1, 42–4)

Then, at the termination of the wooing-scene, comes 'And yet to win her, all the world to nothing' (I, 2, 238). It's a wager, essentially a wager with himself. The soliloquy is basically incredulous, as the largely serious tone of the first part indicates. 'And will she yet debase her eyes on me?' He cannot believe in his own success (any more than he does later). So he turns it into a jest, and formalises, to himself, the wager: 'My dukedom to a beggarly denier, / I do mistake my person all this while.' (I, 2, 252–3) But there is no mistake; and not even the apparent triumph of the gamester can conceal his incapacity to believe in himself, or his success. 'Since I am crept in favour with myself . . .' Ultimately, the wager will be lost. When he comes to 'play the touch' it is a kind of hazard. There is, as he realises, a further chance of failure, that Buckingham will not be 'current gold'. His perception of Buckingham is that of a co-rider in a long, cross-country race, perhaps a hunt: 'Hath he so long held out with me untired, / And stops he now for breath?' (IV, 2, 44–5) The metaphor is left unelaborated, but the idea is of challenge and risk. And the metaphor suggests a further point: the nominal finishing-post has now been passed, but Richard cannot pull up. The race, and not the prize (or quarry) is what matters. The unseen horse who is the only true 'neighbour to my counsels' is with him here, as at the last. It is the motive power of Richard's course, the figure for the demonic energy of the rider. The most famous actor's cry in Shakespeare is, then, an entirely logical climax to Richard's life:

> Slave, I have set my life upon a cast,
> And I will stand the hazard of the die:
> I think there be six Richmonds in the field –
> Five have I slain today instead of him.
> My horse! a horse! My kingdom for a horse!

This means a good deal more than the simple sense that Richard risks his own life through fighting in the field. Taken in conjunction with the network of playing/gaming terms, it suggests that only in hazarding can he satisfy himself. To exist, is to venture. And to succeed, is merely to have negotiated a further phase in a sustained gaming operation; which will continue until he has finally gambled away his life. So 'die' is the conclusive pun of *Richard III*; and the cry for a horse is that of the gamester in extremis, the last appeal for funds to make one more throw.

III

'Play', then, is in the widest sense the verb that accounts for Richard, and his history. I want now to return to some of the more orthodox and readily accessible implications of 'play', those relating to a dramatic performance. It is evident that Richard feels himself to be starring in a private drama, and that this sense of theatre is heightened during the phase in which Buckingham becomes his fellow actor. On this, Emrys Jones has some excellent comments:

> It is in this last phase of his climb to royal power (III, 5, to III, 7) that Shakespeare devises a sequence so extravagantly histrionic in conception as to seem like a half-acknowledged play-within-a-play. The theatrical metaphor is certainly in Shakespeare's – and Richard's – mind:
>
> *Glos.* Come, cousin, canst thou quake and change thy colour,
> Murder thy breath in middle of a word,
> And then again begin, and stop again,
> As if thou were distraught and mad with terror?
> *Buck.* Tut, I can counterfeit the deep tragedian;
> Speak and look back, and pry on every side,
> Tremble and start at wagging of a straw,
> Intending deep suspicion . . .
>
> (III, 5, 1–8)
>
> And the sequence that follows till the end of the act has a peculiarly heightened, histrionic intensity. This is largely because in earlier scenes Richard had usually been the sole 'actor'; he had assumed roles hypocritically and played them before audiences ignorant of the deception. But now he has engaged Buckingham as a fellow actor, and this establishes the atmosphere of true theatricality: a group-assumption of roles devised and rehearsed beforehand.[16]

Much of what passes during this sequence, then, is a series of actors' in-jokes. Thus, Buckingham's 'Had you not come upon your cue, my lord, / William Lord Hastings had pronounced your part' (III, 4, 27–8) is a peculiarly Shakespearean vibration: 'cue' and 'part' are at once metaphor and actuality, leaving the immediate audience to take it in whatever sense it wishes. Essentially it is meant for Richard, but others present will know how to understand it; Ely is scarcely deceived, as 'Your Grace, we think, should soonest know his mind' indicates (III, 4, 9). All this is superb comedy. But then follows IV, 2, and 'Stand all apart' with its jarring proclamation that a different sort of drama is upon the audience. The challenge to criticism is to account, aesthetically, for the break, to demonstrate that Shakespeare is writing a genuinely one-part play (with, if you like, an interval) and not two prolonged Acts rather clumsily stitched together. It is unnecessary and unworthy to adopt the latter account. I propose a simple version: Richard's encounter with reality begins not in IV,[2] (that is merely the point at which the dramatist makes us aware of a 'foregone conclusion') but in III, 7:

Glos. How now, my lord, what say the citizens?
Buck. Now, by the holy mother of our Lord,
The citizens are mum, speak not a word.
(III, 7, 1–3)

Buckingham elaborates. No detail has been spared to bring the citizens to a proper understanding of the matter:

And when mine oratory grew to an end
I bid them that did love their country's good
Cry 'God save Richard, England's royal king!'
Glos. Ah! and did they so?
Buck. No, so God help me, they spake not a word...
(III, 7, 20–4)

What will it profit an actor to star in his own monodrama, if the audience refuse to applaud? The truth is that Richard has failed in the moment of his apparent triumph. The public, the only audience for the Actor-King, will have none of him. It is fear, and not conviction, that makes them submit. Force, not reasoning, accounts for Cardinal Bourchier's volte-face, 'My lord, you shall o'er-rule my mind for once' (III, 1, 57): fear animates the Scrivener's 'Yet who's so bold that says he sees it not?' (III, 6, 12): and it is prudence, not credulity, that inclines the Mayor (like his humbler fellow-citizens) to compliance: 'But, my good lord, your grace's word shall serve, / As well as I had seen and heard him speak' (III, 5, 62–3). To regard the entire dramatis personae in the first half as Richard's gulls is a complete mis-reading (identical, of course, with Richard's own).[17] The only real candidates are Anne, the bovine Hastings, and perhaps the sick Edward. Clarence's subconscious is not deceived, as the dream attests; Stanley and the Queen's circle know him well; the citizens have a secure grasp of the truth. People are not sure how far he will go, nor can they judge accurately the drift of his latest manœuvrings, but they are well aware of the realities behind the posturings, 'your interior hatred, / Which in your outward actions shows itself' as Queen Elizabeth puts it (I, 3, 65–6). It is a society cowed by a single monomaniac in high places. And this, strangely, is the reality that Richard fails to perceive. Obsessed, like Buckingham, with his private theatricals, he fails to note that the audience is too apprehensive to barrack. But of its nature, this particular theatrical requires a participating audience at the crowning moment – King, by acclamation. And there is no applause, no acclamation, merely an embarrassed silence and a shuffling of feet. The real truth then begins to penetrate. For there are no kings without acclamation. Rulers, certainly: but a species of legitimisation is conferred by the consent and applause of the audience/public. Edward, for all his faults, had it. Richard, for all his virtues (and they are genuine) has not. He is a fake, a Not-King, an actor who looks up from the joys of triumphant technique to encounter the stony faces of the audience and the realisation that the community, which alone can confer kingship, is withholding it. That is the true anagnorisis of the play, the moment that leads to the formally elaborated anagnorisis of the Act V soliloquy. And that soliloquy, as we shall see, is purely an encounter with a department of self, the conscience; and what is the conscience but a kind of audience? The sullen mass of the commonalty in III, 7, the herds summoned by the Justices to act as extras in the charade of the Ricardian coup d'état, are the audience that supply the figure for conscience, for *knowing*, in Richard's moral progress.

IV

The central fact of III, 7, then, is the collapse of the scaffolding around Richard's psychic position, while leaving the main structure apparently intact and triumphant. Richard has been curiously protected throughout the first part. I point to the fact that he has not needed to violate the taboo on killing the King. Edward is sick and dying, hence Richard has been able to wait on events there; a primary taboo has been shielded from his consciousness. His general luck has been startling. But now the rigged election lights on Richard, and he has to meet a situation for which he is not mentally prepared at all. The actor has to play *and be* King, has to fuse role and essence. The task proves psychologically impossible. He is, as he realises surrounded by enemies. No doubt this is objectively true: even paranoids, as one says, have real enemies. But his suspicions create realities out of his fears. And so the second half of the play is a prolonged confrontation between Richard and the realities that he had evaded. It becomes a sustained examination of Richard's *self*, conducted by events and personified in Queen Elizabeth.

'Self' is a concept beyond the compass of this book, perhaps any; it is here only necessary to identify Shakespeare's sense of the term. He clearly envisages 'self', as the final soliloquy demonstrates, as the participants in a dialogue. There is the 'self' that one projects upon the world, and the inner 'self' that is related to, perhaps responsible for, the outer 'self' but which is in essence separate from it. The outer self is an appendage to 'person', the person that disgusts Richard's inner self:

> Then, since this world affords no joy to me,
> But to command, to check, to o'erbear such
> As are of better person than myself...
> (*3 Henry VI*, III, 2, 165–7)

The inner self recoils always from the reminder of what the outer is not. Thus, the genuine amazement at Anne's yielding: 'Hath she forgot already that brave prince? . . . A sweeter and a lovelier gentleman . . . The spacious world cannot again afford' (I, 2, 240–6). Thus, the recognition of young York's qualities:

> O, 'tis a parlous boy;
> Bold, quick, ingenious, forward, capable:
> He's all the mother's, from the top to toe.
> (III, 1, 154–6)

Richard has been struck home, yet there's no impulse to blame York (as Buckingham does, apparently in anticipation of Richard's rage); there's a note almost of regret here. The handsome Edward represents the self that Richard cannot encompass, hence 'And therefore, since I cannot prove a lover, / . . . I am determined to prove a villain.' It is a second best, as 'crept in favour with myself' concedes. Nevertheless, the outer self has great success for three Acts, and the inner is acquiescent. But there is an edge to his response to Buckingham: 'My other self, my counsel's consistory, / My oracle, my prophet!' (II, 2, 151–2). One actor is enough. Is there not a trace of irritation here at the presence of the alter ego? The tone of the response (which is essentially a change of mode) implies a kind of rejection, a self-reservation. And in Act IV the joys of role-playing have diminished. There is, for instance, the conclusion to the IV, 2 reflections :

> Murder her brothers, and then marry her !
> Uncertain way of gain ! But I am in
> So far in blood that sin will pluck on sin :
> Tear-falling pity dwells not in this eye.
> (IV, 2, 63–6)

The final line is almost a sententia. He's *reminding* himself of the role now, of what the performance entails. Still more interesting is the conclusion to the IV, 3 soliloquy. Since it must be supposed that Richard is as capable as the audience of remembering his own lines, we can regard him as aware of the resonance in 'To her go I, a jolly thriving wooer' (IV, 3, 43). It's a moody recognition that he who could not prove a lover must now be a wooer. (It is also, as I judge, the last of the soliloquies that can be regarded as direct address to a mental audience.) The joke is on Richard : which is why, simply and centrally, we may if we wish designate the play a comedy. Act IV, Scene 4 now turns into an extended examination of Richard, in the guise of a colloquy on the precise implications of *wooer*. Queen Elizabeth's mockery of the marriage proposition leads to :

> *K. Rich.* Come, come, you mock me; this is not the way
> To win your daughter.
> *Q. Eliz.* There is no other way;
> Unless thou could put on some other shape,
> And not be Richard that hath done all this.
> (IV, 4, 284–7)

His attempts to swear are successively broken down, until

> *K. Rich.* Then by myself –
> *Q. Eliz.* Thyself thyself misusest.
> (IV, 4, 376)

Thus, Richard's culminating 'myself myself confound' (299) is at once a parallel to Buckingham's false oath, and a literal statement of the irreparable harm he has done himself. All this is formalised in the final soliloquy before Bosworth :

> What do I fear? myself? there's none else by :
> Richard loves Richard; that is, I am I.

> Is there a murderer here? No. Yes, I am:
> Then fly. What, from myself? Great reason why:
> Lest I revenge. What, myself upon myself:
> Alack, I love myself. Wherefore? for any good
> That I myself have done unto myself?
> O, no! alas, I rather hate myself
> For hateful deeds committed by myself.
> I *am* a villain...
> I shall despair. There is no creature loves me;
> And if I die, no soul shall pity me:
> Nay, wherefore should they, since that I myself
> Find in myself no pity to myself?
> (v, 3, 182–91, 200–3)

It is the inexorably logical outcome of the error indicated in *3 Henry VI*, and rehearsed in the opening soliloquy to *Richard III*. Richard's attempt to live at peace with himself through the adoption of a role is after all a delusion. The inner dialogue has yielded the same product as the external dialogue with the inquisitor, Queen Elizabeth. (This, and not the 'wooing' duplication which distresses so many commentators, is the point of the scene.) The final threnody on 'self' is, then, the terminal refutation of 'I am myself alone' (*3 Henry VI*, v, 6, 83). And the address to the troops we can read as a kind of epilogue, a recognition that the role is, after all, all that is left. The Bad King Richard has his apotheosis here, in the superbly cynical appeal to the sexual and racial feelings of the soldiery. The alternative to a private hell is a variant of 'bustle':

> Our strong arms be our conscience, swords our law.
> March on, join bravely, let us to 't pell-mell;
> If not to heaven, then hand in hand to hell.
> (v, 3, 311–13)

That is it, and there is great insight to the old stage-tradition tag here, older it may be than Colley Cibber, as old perhaps as Shakespeare: 'Richard's himself again.'[18]

V

That is one way of reading the second half of *Richard III*, by seeing it as Richard's encounter with the realities of an abused self. But the personal history of Richard is set against a larger history, a dramatised meditation on truth and record. A few related terms mutate softly into each other in the evolution of the play; and they supply their own commentary on the situation of Richard.

There is scarcely a real narrative or chronology to these terms, but certain phases of the play do emphasize one or other of them. We can begin with the nominal identification of self, *house*. There is much talk of house and rank in the early scenes. The play's second line, for instance, refers to the triumph of York. Richard's dialogue with Clarence contains a contemptuous rejection of the upstart kinsmen of the Queen; and this class antagonism is the theme of the I, 3 bickering, 'Yea, and much more; but I was born so high' (262), continued into the ironic descending arpeggio of 'Dukes, earls, lords, gentlemen; indeed, of all' (II, 1, 68). But title, in Brackenbury's elegy over the sleeping Clarence, modulates into a *de contemptu mundi*:

> Princes have but their titles for their glories . . .
> So that, betwixt their titles and low name,
> There's nothing differs but the outward fame.
> (I, 4, 78–83)

Title, in this sense, minors the triumph of III, 7, and

> Then I salute you with this kingly title:
> Long live Richard, England's royal king!
> (III, 7, 239–40)

In context, 'title' is immediately ironic. So Richard's questioning of his own title – it is virtually his first act as king – is a logical extension of the questions implicit in the earlier text:

> But shall we wear these honours for a day?
> Or shall they last, and we rejoice in them?
> (IV, 2, 5–6)

Thus Richard launches the overt challenge to 'title'. The function passes to Queen Elizabeth, but only after she has endured her own challenge from Queen Margaret, in the *ubi sunt* set-piece of IV, 4:

> I called thee then poor shadow, painted queen,
> The presentation of but what I was,
> The flattering index of a direful pageant . . .
> A queen in jest, only to fill the scene . . .
> (IV, 4, 83–5, 91)

'Shadow', 'painted', 'pageant', 'scene' point to the play metaphor, as also to 'title'. It is, in the terms of poetic drama, a spiritual ordeal that Queen Elizabeth is subjected to; and it invests with greater authority her dissection of Richard:

> Under what title shall I woo for thee . . . ?
> But how long shall that title 'ever' last?
> (IV, 4, 340, 350)

Titles, significantly, now fill Richard's life. Catesby manages three in two lines, and Catesby would know what his master wants to hear:

> First, mighty liege, tell me your highness' pleasure,
> What from your grace I shall deliver to him.
> (V, 4, 446–7)

Bosworth itself is presented as a challenge to title. The Royalist forces have a three-to-one majority.

> Besides, the King's name is a tower of strength,
> Which they upon the adverse party want.
> (V, 3, 12–13)

The failure of 'title' is thus actualised in the course of battle. The victory is not simply a lucky chance for the minority, but a predetermined outcome in which the Breton forces figure *conscience*:

> *Oxford* Every man's conscience is a thousand swords,
> To fight against this bloody homicide.
> (V, 2, 17–18)

And 'title' itself is simply an outgrowth of history, a product of the record. *Record* is a strangely insistent term. Prince Edward, in his meditation on the Tower, raises the issues:

> *Prince Ed.* Is it upon record, or else reported
> Successively from age to age, he built it?
> *Buckingham* But say, my lord, it were not register'd.
> Methinks the truth should live from age to age,
> As 'twere retail'd to all posterity,
> Even to the general all-ending day.
> (III, 1, 72–8)

The matter has no narrative point whatsoever; yet Shakespeare is never so much himself as when apparently digressing. The young Prince is musing, as the play muses, upon the antitheses of truth and historical legend, of record and mere report. The same vibrations, as with a tuning-fork, are struck with the *Recorder* of III, 7, the magistrate whose function is to mediate between Buckingham's fraudulences and the people. He symbolises the distinction between mere 'report' and the truth. Richard, naturally, reserves 'record' for his own purposes :

> Made him my book, wherein my soul recorded
> The history of all her secret thoughts :
> (III, 5, 27–8)

This exploitation of history (in its usual sense) remains constant right up to the final address to the troops, in which he engagingly asserts the Bretons to be bastards of the English : 'And, on record, left them the heirs of shame' (v, 335). The best instance of Richard's usage occurs earlier, however. The lamenting queens are threatened with

> Either be patient, and entreat me fair,
> Or with the clamorous report of war
> Thus will I drown your exclamations.
> IV, 4, 151–3)

'Report' is a superbly apt pun here : it combines the idea of the sound of cannon, and the version of history that the military victors will impose.

'Record' comprehends also the attempt in Act III to rewrite history. The Scrivener tells us of his labours in writing history (Hastings' indictment) in advance of events : it is political theatre. The chief architect of the falsified record is Buckingham, whose speeches even rewrite the Yorkist genealogy ('by just computation of the time'). It is worth digressing here to consider Buckingham's style in relation to falsified history. His mode is a cloying, fulsome public rhetoric. Thus, before the mourning Court :

> You cloudy princes and heart-sorrowing peers,
> That bear this mutual heavy load of moan . . .
> (II, 2, 109–10)

or

> You are too senseless-obstinate, my lord,
> Too ceremonious and traditional :
> Weigh it but with the grossness of this age,
> You break not sanctuary in seizing him.
> (III, 1, 44–7)

This is the end of the ceremonial of *1 Henry VI*, that period – aeons past – when the good Duke Humphrey was so shocked at a letter bearing the superscription 'To the King'. The collapse of values is also a collapse of language, for here the brutality of the argument, combined with the ersatz sweetening of the reasoning, is singularly unpleasant. Buckingham's language is curiously imprinted with this Official Version quality; it reads at times like an Elizabethan document for Orwell's 'Politics and the English Language'; it is unusual for events to compel him to the simplicity of 'My lord, whoever journeys to the prince, / For God's sake, let not us two be behind'. Even in conference with Richard and Catesby, the public euphemisms rise readily:

> What think'st thou? is it not an easy matter
> To make William Lord Hastings of our mind,
> For the instalment of this noble duke
> In the seat royal of this famous isle?
>
> (III, 1, 161–4)

The diction of the last two lines is fascinating, and disturbing. It is, after all, a coup d'état that Buckingham is talking about. Perhaps it's heavy, self-conscious irony, perhaps a habit of talking that even a conspirator finds hard to discard. (Buckingham does not have the excuse that Catesby does, in the following scene, for his delicate allusion to the 'garland of the realm'.) Whatever the psychological justification here, Buckingham's language is completely a part of the play. It is a distillation of the public lie that is everywhere in *Richard III*.

VI

'Record' cannot, however, stray too far from the idea of *time*. The ancient Duchess of York has this awareness, in her self-epitome as 'brief abstract and record of tedious days' (IV, 4, 28). Time is the force that discovers and defeats Richard. The application is implicit in Queen Margaret's apostrophe, to Queen Elizabeth: 'Thus hath the course of justice wheel'd about, / And left thee but a very prey to time . . .' (IV, 4, 105–6). Queen Elizabeth passes it on, as she does with much else from the elder queen, to Richard: 'That thou has wronged in the time o'er past' and so on, in a passage which iterates 'time' on five occasions within a few lines (IV, 4, 388–96). It defeats Richard's attempt to swear by 'The time to come' (IV, 4, 387).

And *time* emerges in that most simple of all concretisations, *clock*. Throughout the second part of the play, Richard is asking for the time. It is a tic, almost. Buckingham's interruption meets

K. Rich. Ay, what's o'clock?
Buck. I am thus bold to put your grace in mind
Of what you promised me.
K. Rich. Well, but what's o'clock?
Buck. Upon the stroke of ten.
K. Rich. Well, let it strike.
Buck. Why let it strike?
K. Rich. Because that, like a Jack, thou keep'st the stroke
Betwixt thy begging and my meditation.
(IV, 2, 112–18

Buckingham, the 'Jack' on the outside of the clock, is the importunate and intolerable reminder of the claims of time. The obscure reference to 'Humphrey Hour' (IV, 4, 175) presumably relates to the same point. Again, on the eve of Bosworth, 'What is't o'clock?' (V, 3, 47) 'Give me a watch' (V, 3, 63), which has two obvious meanings, is presumably another strategic ambiguity since both are relevant. Finally, 'Tell the clock there. Give me a calendar' is Richard's welcoming of the day of Bosworth. (V, 3, 276) It is evident that Shakespeare means to fix the portrait of a man obsessed with the passage of time (and who, originally, had 'no delight to pass away the time'). All details matter in Shakespeare; and perhaps the best way of characterising Richard is, in Queen Elizabeth's phrase, 'a prey to time'.

The presence that emerges towards the close of *Richard III*, then, and which articulates the action, is time. For Richard, time is the refutation of a life of role-playing. The 'shadows' that visit him on the eve of Bosworth complete the play metaphor, for 'shadow' can mean 'actor' as well as 'spirit'.[19] So the minor players in Richard's triumph return as audience to his fall. For Richmond, time is history; which is a way of saying that history becomes Richmond. The closing speech is the new record, the prophecy that time has endorsed. In dramatic context, the effect of Richmond's triumph is complete and unarguable. The spirit of irony, for the first time in the play, is decorously absent. Still, the challenge to *title* and *record* is latent, coded, in the cells of this play. But 1592 or so is too soon for a revisionist historian of 1485.

2 *King John:* Some Bastards Too

The problems of *King John* invite a direct confrontation: what is the play about? For Tillyard, it is about 'the theory of loyalty and when it is lawful to rebel against the reigning king.'[1] Irving Ribner, in the same vein, recognises the 'political didacticism' of *King John*: Faulconbridge's decision is 'The orthodox doctrine Shakespeare wishes to present most dramatically: Faulconbridge will serve the *de facto* king, unlawful and sinful though he be, for rebellion, the worst of evils, could only further anger God, whereas lawful submission might cause God to effect a reformation in the king.'[2] Sigurd Burckhardt sees a totally different play: 'What *King John* presents us with is a world in which authority is totally untrustworthy.'[3] These commentators identify the same area of subject-matter (authority and rebellion) but adopt differing perspectives on the issues. While inclining to Burckhardt's view of *King John*, I do not regard any of these formulations as wholly satisfactory. The play cannot be crudely didactic, because John's treatment of Arthur is fully exposed as a human and political crime; there are limits to the obedience a King can exact of a subject, and the play explores them. But however 'untrustworthy' authority may be, it exists, and the subject has few options to exercise. The play offers a perplexing analysis of the nature of authority in relation to right, and opts finally for a situation (based on the value of the nation-state) which actors and audience can agree on as inevitable and right. To that extent only does *King John* appear to me didactic, in that it grounds itself finally on the enduring values of community and collective Government (it is clear that young Henry will have to rely very considerably on his Cabinet).[4] The controlling metaphor for the issues of right and authority is bastardy, together with legitimacy; and these issues are best realised through analysis by phases of the play's organisation.

I

The opening movement of *King John* extends to the end of Act II. It is, in effect, a dramatisation of the concept of 'right'. As E. A. J.

Honigmann remarks, the play often exhibits a dualism of value-systems, and 'The middle star in this galaxy of elaborated concepts emerges, finally, as the age-old will-o'-the-wisp of right and wrong, or right and might.'[5] But the concepts originate from a single heavily-emphasised word; and two-thirds of the play's references to 'right' occur in I, 1 and II, 1. Its usage in *King John* exploits the word's primary quibble of meaning, for 'right' comprehends moral and legal justice. The adjective tends to assert the force of moral, and the noun of legal. And the action of the drama points up the distinction, for the term 'right' virtually launches the play:

Chatillon Philip of France, in right and true behalf
Of thy deceased brother Geoffrey's son,
Arthur Plantagenet, lays most lawful claim
To this fair island and the territories: . . .
And put the same into young Arthur's hand,
Thy nephew and right royal sovereign.
K. John What follows if we disallow of this?
Chatillon The proud control of fierce and bloody war,
To enforce these rights so forcibly withheld.
(I, 1, 7–18)

These are the public statements. Eleanor and John discuss the issue, a moment later, in private.

K. John Our strong possession and our right for us.
Eleanor Your strong possession much more than your right,
Or else it must go wrong with you and me:
So much my conscience whispers in your ear,
Which none but heaven and you and I shall hear.
(I, 1, 39–43)

Thus a central doubt is cast upon public 'right'. The doubt springs from the formal opposition of claims – there can be no absolute truth here – and from the explicit weakness that Eleanor and John concede in England's claim. And the erratic and self-interested behaviour of the principals does little to validate their claims. 'Right' belongs to the category of words that are contained *within* a Shakespeare play, rather than serve as external facts to which the text merely alludes. It is, in part, the function of this play to parse, to dramatise, and to question 'right' as a concept of public action.

It is not necessary to elaborate the point into the formal details of the prolonged Anglo-French quarrel in Acts I and II. Much more interesting is the (very Shakespearean) dimension of the analysis that Act I supplies. Following the public exchange between John and

Chatillon, the play moves to the domestic claims of the Faulconbridges. This scene, as presented in *King John*, is a mutation of the opening: 'legitimacy' succeeds 'right'. Now this is strictly true of *The Troublesome Raigne of John King of England* too, for the Bastard episode does indeed follow immediately upon Chatillon's embassy. But the author of the *Troublesome Raigne* appears to have no real grasp of the possibilities of his material here. France's claim is presented as a simple ultimatum; the word 'right' is never mentioned in the scene; Shakespeare's dialogue between John and Eleanor, establishing the weakness of England's claim, has no counterpart in the *Troublesome Raigne*. The human interest of the Faulconbridges is played up, the political ironies of the Anglo-French contention played down. Hence the episodes merely follow each other in the *Troublesome Raigne*. If, as most critics believe, Shakespeare reworked the material of the older play here, this furnishes a classic instance of what Shakespeare brings to pre-existent material. The anonymous author has no idea of the gold he has thrown up, whereas Shakespeare has discerned the central possibility in the source. His perception is of bastardy as the metaphoric vehicle for political right and wrong, together with the role of the Bastard as the voice of challenge to the disputants in the major action. In Shakespeare, then, the consecutive episodes relate to a central core of meaning.

The Bastard's entirely complementary relationship with King John is, as everyone sees, the structure of the play in personal terms.[6] It is more than that. The idea of the play is that the Bastard embodies the critique of public affairs which are themselves conducted (largely) by King John. John asserts a fiction (at best, a doubtful legalism) to be a reality, the English claim to the territories in France: The Bastard discards a fiction, and affirms a reality.

Bastard But, mother, I am not Sir Robert's son:
I have disclaim'd Sir Robert and my land;
Legitimation, name, and all is gone . . .
Lady F. Hast thou denied thyself a Faulconbridge?
Bastard As faithfully as I deny the devil.
(I, 1, 246–52)

The Bastard is the voice of reality in *King John*; it is a function that elsewhere Shakespeare allots to his Clowns and to women. He is the jester, the commentator, the critic. He even turns himself into a metaphor, an intellectual feat of great agility: 'For he is but a bastard to the time / That doth not smack of observation' (I, 1, 207–8). That is Shakespeare's hint, plainly enough; and we ought to see Faulconbridge, as we see the Fools generally, as Shakespeare's stalking horse in the play.

The Bastard's major opportunity occurs in II, 1. Formally, the scene is an extended dispute over 'right' (the word occurs eighteen times here) together with 'legitimacy' and 'justice'. In response to the counter-claims of John and Philip, the citizens of Angiers acknowledge the sovereignty of England but prudently refrain from identifying its ruler :

Hubert In brief, we are the king of England's subjects :
For him, and in his right, we hold this town.
K. John Acknowledge then the king, and let me in.
Hubert That can we not; but he that proves the king,
To him will we prove loyal;
(II, 1, 267–71)

The satiric vein is even stronger in Hubert's later rejoinder to the expostulating kings :

K. Philip Speak, Citizens, for England; who's your king?
Hubert The king of England, when we know the king.
(II, 1, 362–3)

But what energises the formal dispute is the presence of the Bastard, that living metaphor. To say that he incarnates (in this scene especially) the images of sexual congress is too crude. He does, however, act as a kind of magnetic field to which these images tend to direct themselves. In part, the sexual images are related to the literal status of political legitimacy as based on marital fidelity; in part, they extend the concept beyond the literal. Thus, Philip charges John with having 'outfaced infant state, and done a rape / Upon the maiden virtue of the crown.' (II, 1, 97–8) This is clearly a metaphor, as is 'To look into the blots and stains of right' (II, 1, 114), yet a moment later the charges have emerged as literal :

Eleanor Who is it thou dost call usurper, France?
Constance Let me make answer; thy usurping son.
Eleanor Out, insolent! Thy bastard shall be king,
That thou mayst be a queen, and check the world!
Constance My bed was ever to thy son as true
As thine was to thy husband; . . .
My boy a bastard! By my soul, I think
His father never was so true begot :
It cannot be, an if thou wert his mother.
Eleanor There's a good mother, boy, that blots thy father.
Constance There's a good grandam, boy, that would blot thee.
(II, 1, 120–33)

'Bastard', originally the word of the minor action, is now assimilated into the major. The last lines cited above emphasise the point, for they parallel Lady Faulconbridge's 'Where is that slave, thy brother? where is he, / That holds in chase mine honour up and down?' (I, 1, 222–3) The language of the later passage, then, makes a unity of the figurative and the literal. But it is still the Bastard who enforces the idea into the audience's mind. He does so in this remarkable brace of interventions:

K. John Doth not the crown of England prove the king?
And if not that, I bring you witnesses,
Twice fifteen thousand hearts of England's breed, –
Bastard Bastards and else.
K. John To verify our title with their lives.
K. Phil. As many and as well-born bloods as those, –
Bastard Some bastards too.
K. Phil. Stand in his face to contradict his claim.
(II, 1, 273–80)

Six words, and most of the play with them. The English bear, as Chatillon had earlier warned, 'Their birthrights proudly on their backs' (II, 1, 70): but here the play detaches itself equally from the rhetoric of Philip ('God and our right!' II, 1, 335). The derisive marginalia of the Bastard states an ancient truth: that claimants to legitimacy had best come with harness on their backs.

When, therefore, the Bastard greets the sudden accommodation of the disputants with a disbelieving 'Mad world! mad kings! mad composition!' (II, 561–98), this is no sudden set-piece of rhetoric. It is a distillation of everything that has gone before, a conclusion that cannot be separated from its premises. Even the central metaphors of the speech pick up the imagery of sexual congress, for Commodity is seen as a seducer (571–3) and a bawd (582). 'Right', at this stage of the play, is seen as public relations for 'Commodity'. The refutation appears complete, and the Bastard's conversion to 'gain' is a crude, but organic, realisation of the preceding action.

II

The second movement of *King John* I take to extend from III, 1 to the end of Act IV. It traces the consequences of the Anglo-French accord, and can be thought of as an evolving analysis of 'right'. But the mode of experience passes from *claim* to *doubt*. Uncertainty is now the central experience of *King John*; and it is expressed, above all, in the Bastard's 'I am amaz'd' speech that concludes the movement.

The current of the play flows, in III, 1, through Constance. Her diatribe expresses above all incredulity: 'It is not so . . . it cannot be . . . Believe me, I do not believe thee, man:' (III, 1, 4–9). To her, for a moment, the role of critic of the great passes. Her critique is fully realised in the 'forsworn' speech of III, 1, 99–112. It points to the deepening complications of the play: Philip is in a genuine difficulty, made much worse by the intervention of Pandulph. Through him, the mutation of 'right' becomes 'lawful':

Pandulph There's law and warrant, lady, for my curse.
Constance And for mine too: when law can do no right
Let it be lawful that law bar no wrong:
Law cannot give my child his kingdom here,
For he that holds his kingdom holds the law;
Therefore, since law itself is perfect wrong,
How can the law forbid my tongue to curse?
(III, 1, 184–90)

The clash of imperatives, which is the essence of politics, is now manifest. It is, then, the recurring situation of this movement that Philip voices: 'I am perplex'd, and know not what to say.' (III, 1, 221) The elements of that perplexity are detailed in

K. Phil. I may disjoin my hand, but not my faith.
Pandulph So makest thou faith an enemy to faith,
And like a civil war set'st oath to oath,
Thy tongue against thy tongue.
(III, 1, 262–5)

And Pandulph's speech (III, 1, 263–97), an intricacy of rhetoric and paradox, makes the 'perplexity' seem more founded: he too, is the play. And so the matter is again put to the test of arms, the outcome of which is Arthur's capture by John. So far the play's problems, though bafflingly refractory in Act III, have been essentially technical, i.e., confined to the realm of political calculation and manœuvre, military power, and legality. But now the problems focus to a concrete moral issue, the fate of Arthur. The scenes of John's hooded injunction to Hubert (III, 3) and the abortive blinding (IV, 1) are what everybody remembers of this play; they are the supreme theatrical events of *King John*. They expound, however, with an implacable organic logic, the development of the drama from its earliest moments. The simple France v. England confrontation of the opening passage appears now as a political age of innocence. The play has evolved, through the deepening complications of Act III, to the blinding of an innocent boy. And each action has been the outcome of a felt political imperative. There are no evildoers in *King John* : only evil. John himself, as deeply perplexed as any, never loses his status as a morally aware human being:

> There is no sure foundation set on blood,
> No certain life achieved by others' death.
> (IV, 2, 104–5)

He comes, then, to the self-refutation of

> It is the curse of kings to be attended
> By slaves that take their humours for a warrant
> To break within the bloody house of life,
> And on the winking of authority
> To understand a law, to know the meaning
> Of dangerous majesty, when perchance it frowns
> More upon humour than advised respect.
> (IV, 2, 208–14)

'To understand a law' is a supreme irony. 'Law' as we have seen, is the variant of 'right'; and the capacity to understand a law is precisely the claim of the kings throughout this play. The perspective of *King John* reduces the king to his subject, and the self-refutation of the monarch merges with the larger refutation of the play.

Uncertainty remains the dominant note. It is expressed, for instance, by Hubert ('My Lord?' III, 2, 66), by Pembroke ('And I do fearfully believe 'tis done, / What we so fear'd he had a charge to do', IV, 2, 74–5), and by John himself as he interrogates Hubert concerning the portents governing the French invasion ('Five moons?' IV, 2, 185). It appears generally in the reactions of the English lords to Arthur's death. This is a simple affair in the *Troublesome Raigne.* The body is found, Hubert protests his innocence, and is forthwith believed. Here, the situation is lengthened out to express the continuing experience of incredulity (precisely what Constance began the movement with, in III, 1). The seven 'ifs' that occur between IV, 3, 59–135 are the vectors by which we can note the direction of the dramatic energies. Above all, they are transmitted through the Bastard, the signpost of mood and direction; and the reduction of the second movement is 'I am amaz'd, methinks, and lose my way, / Among the thorns and dangers of this world' (IV, 3, 140–1).

III

The final Act, the play's third movement, is the main challenge to Shakespeare's art. He has to produce some kind of intellectually and emotionally satisfying resolution to the piercing dilemmas of *King John*. Or to put the matter differently, he has to write in a justification for the speech which we know will end the play, and which has so often been regarded as an essentially evasive piece of jingoism, designed to conceal with curtain-plaudits the lameness of the conclusion. That is the critic's challenge, too. What, then, is the case for 'Come the three corners of the world in arms, / And we shall shock them'?

The case begins much earlier: with the play's opening line, if you like; 'Now say, Chatillon, what would France with us?' This inaugurates the concern with the identification of nation and king. 'France' and 'England' are freely used as synecdoche for 'The King of France' and 'The King of England'. There is, in the early passages, no reason to regard this customary usage as dramatically important. The bland equivalence of nation and king begins, perhaps to appear a little less than innocent with the monarchs' reply to the citizen's 'Who is it that hath warn'd us to the walls?'

K. Phil. 'Tis France, for England.
K. John England, for itself.
(II, 1, 201–2)

The claim, presented with a degree of ironic detachment by the playwright, casts doubt upon the claimants. That, indeed, is the force of the entire play. The self-definitions of John and Philip are seen ultimately as absurd:

K. John What earthy name to interrogatories
Can taste the free breath of a sacred king?
(III, 1, 147–8)

The events of v, 1 – John receives his crown back from the Pope's emissary – form a sufficient answer to that. Lewis' reversal is quicker:

Lewis Look, where the holy legate comes apace,
To give us warrant from the hand of heaven,
And on our actions set the name of right
With holy breath . . .
Your grace shall pardon me, I will not back:
I am too high-born to be propertied,

To be a secondary at control,
Or useful serving-man and instrument
To any sovereign state throughout the world.
(v, 2, 65–8, 78–82)

King John is among other things a clear rejection of the more extreme claims of kings for themselves. But the play proceeds to a more elegiac recognition of the dissociation between king and realm. John has it, in his despair at Hubert's news :

My nobles leave me, and my state is brav'd,
Even at my gates, with ranks of foreign powers :
Nay, in the body of this fleshly land,
This kingdom, this confine of blood and breath,
Hostility and civil tumult reigns
Between my conscience and my cousin's death.
(iv, 2, 243–8)

Classically Shakespearean, this speech moves from the external situation (the war, part invasion and part rebellion) to the perception of the external as a figure for self. England becomes an emblem for John – the reverse of the opening, in which he is the emblem of England. And the evident mortality of kings underlines the subtler querying. 'How easy dost thou take all England up, / From forth this morsel of dead royalty !' muses the Bastard, as Hubert takes up Arthur's corpse. The continuation is interesting :

The life, the right and truth of all this realm
Is fled to Heaven; and England now is left
To tug and scamble, and part by the teeth
The unowed interest of proud swelling state.
(iv, 3, 142–7)

John, certainly, is alive. But when the kings depart, England will be left. And this is now, through Act v, the emerging fact of the drama.

In part, then, the closing stages of *King John* anticipate the concept of 'monarchise', the essential verb of *Richard II*. John, a defeated and ailing husk is in the theatre a defeated idea. Yet he remains the symbol of the realm, and it is to him that Salisbury acknowledges obedience, 'Even to our ocean, to our great King John' (v, 4, 57). The Bastard has no doubt of his duty : it is to make the symbol work. 'Be great in act, as you have been in thought', and so on through a catalogue of excellent advice (v, 1, 45–61). The dissolution of John is nonetheless the narrative line of Act v. But against that line is plotted the rise of that for which John (or 'England') is a name : the realm. Salisbury, in the spiritual agonies of his rebellion, suggests an England with divided identity :

> O nation, that thou couldst remove!
> That Neptune's arms, who clippeth thee about,
> Would bear thee from the knowledge of thyself –
> (v, 2, 33–5)

England, the unchangeable element in the political turmoil, is the basis of the Bastard's harsh rejection of Salisbury and his fellows :

> And you degenerate, you ingrate revolts,
> You bloody Neroes, ripping up the womb
> Of our dear mother England, blush for shame :
> (v, 2, 151–3)

It is to that value that the events of v, 4 are related. The proof of Lewis' treachery refutes the conduct of Salisbury and his allies and Melun himself, reaching out in his dying moments for something to hold fast to, imparts the truth 'For that my grandsire was an Englishman . . .' (v, 4, 42) The play then hurries on to its end.[7] Act v, 6 is an extraordinarily apt theatrical event, a kind of darkness before dawn : Hubert and the Bastard, whispering their signals across the dark ('A friend . . . Of the part of England', v, 6, 2) establish not only the news but a moment of black time in which the future hope is born. It is pure symbolist drama. And the final scene, v, 7, actualises the issues we have considered. John himself, 'a clod / And module of confounded royalty' (v, 7, 57–8) expires in the company of his son and nobility. Prince Henry, 'the cygnet to this pale faint swan' (v, 7, 21), speaks his dirge on the mortality of monarchy, and asks the despairing question : 'What surety of the world, what hope, what stay, / When this was now a king, and now is clay?' (v, 7, 68–9) The question is left in the air for a moment, as the Bastard speaks of following his master; then he reverts to the affairs of State. Salisbury tells of the immediate arrangements that have to be made for the evacuation of the French; the Bastard, followed by the others, makes his submission to the new King; and after Henry's thanks, the Bastard speaks for the last time :

> O, let us pay the time but needful woe,
> Since it hath been beforehand with our griefs.
> This England never did, nor ever shall,
> Lie at the proud foot of a conqueror,
> But when it first did help to wound itself.

Now these her princes are come home again
Come the three corners of the world in arms
And we shall shock them. Nought shall make us rue
If England to itself do rest but true.

Whatever the mortal frailties of monarchs, the King's government must go on. The nation is the ultimate value, and the king now appears as its custodian – not the realm itself. The final move is to pick up the pieces and proceed with the business of State : the matter of England.

The action of *King John* moves through claim and counter-claim, political manœuvre that grows ever wilder, to a resolution born of military disaster. Our experience of *King John* passes from an almost Brechtian alienation in the first movement, through an involvement in the perplexities of the second, to a relieved acquiescence in the solution that the dramatist has conjured up. The first movement might be taken for an exercise in debunking : thereafter nothing is more impressive than the way in which the mounting difficulties of the political situations lead inexorably (as it seems) to their consequences and resolution. And at each stage the Bastard, growing with the play, is present to articulate the interim conclusions. 'Mad world ! mad kings ! . . . I am amaz'd . . . Nought shall make us rue, / If England to itself do rest but true.' The resolution is intellectually stronger than it may appear, for the national is the enemy of the imperial : England is no longer to seek Anjou, Touraine, Maine but consolidate at home. But above all, the primary intellectual tension of 'England' is largely discharged, for the word now commits itself to *realm* rather than *King*. And that distinction, as we have seen, is fundamental to the play. We can think of *King John* as a dramatised analysis of authority and rebellion in relation to right and wrong, whose critical impulse is transmitted through its incarnate metaphor, the Bastard. The force of this analysis is to move from the figurative to the literal, from a kind of illusion to a perceived reality, from 'England' as 'king' to 'England' as *land* – which is, after all, what the word means. The Bastard is not evading the issue, he is stating it. And in kneeling to Prince Henry, he legitimises the custodian and symbol of the land : 'And happily may your sweet self put on / The lineal state and glory of the land !' (v, 7, 101–2).[8] The limitations of the final lines are not those of lameness, but of the provisional. The fuller analysis of nationhood and sovereignty must be deferred. It is left to a minor figure in a later play, an Irishman, to ask the most searching of consequent questions. 'What *is* my nation?' But that is *Henry V* : and another story.

3 *Romeo and Juliet:* The Sonnet-World of Verona

Our general experience of *Romeo and Juliet* is not, I think, an entirely settled matter yet—not settled to the extent that, say, *Macbeth* or *Troilus and Cressida* or *Richard III* is. The play does break sharply into two halves, following the death of Mercutio, and the change of tone and (apparently) direction are marked. We can cope with this, not necessarily crudely, by calling *Romeo and Juliet* a comedy and a tragedy, but the critical problem of unification is not altogether resolved.[1] The central transactions of the play seem to invite a wide range of response. And the language remains an underlying cause of unease, a faint yet unmistakable stimulus and irritant to our responses. Every critic notes that (in Clemen's words) 'the first scenes of *Romeo and Juliet* strike us as more conventional in tone and diction than the later ones.'[2] But what does 'conventional' imply, of approval or disengagement, in this context? How is the partially 'liberated' language of the later events to be taken? How, in brief, does the language of the play guide our responses and imply a judgment?

I

The sonnet is the channel through which the play flows. Acts I and II are preceded by a choric sonnet; Romeo and Juliet at their first encounter compose a sonnet, chimingly, together. Several quatrains and sestets are scattered throughout the play, which closes with the Prince's sestet. Other passages hint broadly at parallels with the Sonnets: Montague's 'Many a morning hath he there been seen, / With tears augmenting the fresh morning's dew', for instance (I, 1, 129–30), and Romeo's 'O she is rich in beauty; only poor, / That, when she dies, with beauty dies her store' (I, 1, 213–14). The sonnet material helps to establish Verona as a country of the mind, a locale whose inhabitants place themselves through their mode of discourse. In the Veronese language, the most obvious adjunct to the sonnet is the rhymed couplet.

It is an easier mode than the cross-rhymes of the sonnet, and the Veronese fall into it naturally. Capulet, for instance, has eleven consecutive rhymed couplets in I, 2, a record which Friar Laurence raises to fifteen in his first scene (II, 3). Romeo himself responds to the Friar in the same mode, and throughout the first half of the play slips easily into rhyme. Rhyme is the shared possession of this society. The Veronese think in rhyme, and communicate in rhyme : Friar Laurence's soliloquy (II, 3) changes not a whit in metre or tone after Romeo's arrival. But rhyme is psychologically more interesting than it looks. I discern two main varieties of the mode. With the elders, the heavy, jogging rhymes have the effect of a self-fulfilling prophecy. *Night* must follow *light* with the same inevitability that it does the day. The rhymes figure a closed system. The younger people, apt to confuse facility with penetration, seize on the other aspect of rhyme—that it can pick up the loose ends of a companion's speech. Thus, to the stimulus of Benvolio's 'I rather weep . . . At thy good heart's oppression', Romeo instantly reacts 'Why such is love's transgression' (I, 1, 181–3). It is a kind of game. The joint composition of the sonnet in I, 5 is, as I take it, a part-conscious event, a tranced process of courtly reciprocity. Juliet's 'You kiss by the book'[8] (I, 5, 110) combines an implied reproach for artificiality, with an acknowledgment of Romeo's dexterity at completing his own (and her) rhymes. Rhyme, in sum, is inward-turning, acquiescent, reflective of social forces. It tends to codify its own categories, and insulate them against erosion. It is Juliet who supplies the best internal comment on all this. Following her parting from Romeo, comes

> *Nurse* What's this, what's this?
> *Juliet* A rhyme I learned even now
> Of one I danced withal.
> (I, 5, 142–3)

So 'rhyme' becomes a kind of crystallisation for the whole episode; a formula for the fluency, the intensity, and the superficiality of the means through which this society orders its experience, and its relationships.

II

The prime effect of the sonnet-material, coupled with this mass of rhyming, is to conduct us into a Petrarchan world. By this I mean a world conceived as a dramatisation of the Elizabethan sonnet collections. The grand cultural allusion that Shakespeare makes is to the explosion of amatory versifying in the early 1590s, a fashion inaugurated by the 'English Petrarke', Sidney. The main facts are well known, but the reader may care to be reminded of the sequence of dates leading up to *Romeo and Juliet*. *Astrophel and Stella* was published in 1591. In 1592. appeared *Delia*, by Samuel Daniel; and *Diana*, by Henry Constable (republished in 1594, with additions). 1593 saw *Parthenophil and Parthenope*, by Barnabe Barnes; *Licia*, by Giles Fletcher; and *Phillis*, by Thomas Lodge. Drayton's *Ideas Mirrour* came out in 1594. 1595 saw the publication of Spenser's *Amoretti*, besides Barnes' *A Divine Centurie of Spirituall Sonnets*. All these are sonnet-sequences, or collections including a large number of sonnets. It is not a complete list, merely an indication that between *Astrophel and Stella* and the composition of *Romeo and Juliet* (that is to say, 1594–6) no year passed without a significant public addition to the effusions of the sonnetteers. For our purposes here, certain characteristics of the sonnet-wave are salient. First, there is a definite acknowledgement of Petrarch himself as the inspiration of the school, and this is occasionally explicit in the verse. Daniel, for instance : 'Though thou a Laura hast no Petrarch found'; and Constable, 'Thy coming to the world hath taught us to descry / What Petrarch's Laura meant . . .'[4] Second, the mode comprises certain personae, attitudes, situations – the cruel mistress, despairing lover, melancholy, insomnia, and so on. Third, the mode is inadequately described as 'conventional'. For several years it was *the* convention, a mental environment that nourished the greatest and smallest : Sidney, Spenser, Shakespeare drew from it the sustenance they needed, as did Fletcher, Barnes, Lodge. All defined themselves in relation to this central convention. Most of its individual exponents are unremarkable. 'Smoothness and standardization, abstractness and unreality, utter lack of criticism or analysis : these are the marks of the lyrical verse which, in the last years of the sixteenth century, was brought against something new.'[5] Shakespeare, however, is in *Romeo and Juliet* using the convention as a means of placing, and implicitly judging, his dramatis personae. J. W. Lever remarks of the minor sonnetteers of the period that 'Like Romeo and Juliet on their first encounter, these poets play delightedly with the conceits of "saints", "pilgrims", "palmers", and "prayers" . . .'[6] Precisely : and this is as true if the comparison is reversed. Romeo and Juliet are playing like minor poets within the current mode. As I take it, Shakespeare is combining an imaginative conception with a ready means of audience communication, for he would expect playgoers to pick up the fashionable expressions of Romeo and his social milieu. He thus combines immediacy of reference with interior, dramatic truth, for the characters assert their life to be exactly of their period. Lever is again à propos here : he reminds us of the extent to which 'life itself is patterned on literary modes : how men in one age tend to conduct their amours in all earnestness, like the heroes of Stendhal; in another, in all flippancy, like the heroes of Noel Coward.'[7] One of the most distinctive features of *Romeo and Juliet* is its almost journalistic flair in identifying the literary movement of the 1590s and the ways in which people modelled themselves upon the movement. Shakespeare's conception, then, synthesises the physical world of Renaissance Italy, the most famous literary expression of that world, and the Elizabethan reception to the expression.

The landscape of *Romeo and Juliet* has a precise inner consistency. It has the curious flatness of a trecento fresco. Not only are there young people and old people; they are young people's old people – and vice versa. The Montagues and Capulets, with their Prince, appear to us as they appear to the lovers – a formal, statuesque frieze of contention and judgement. Neither the Friar nor the Nurse needs a name; they are functionaries, purely. Nobody is middle-aged, nobody is even Hamlet's age. Mercutio aside, no one in the drama is capable of understanding it, and no one does. Nothing could be more indicative of the world the lovers inhabit than the sonnet they speak to each other – that, and the 'Aye me' (predicted by Mercutio) with which Juliet begins her soliloquy. There is no question here of inauthentic emotions (though Romeo, earlier, shows a certain awareness of role-playing). The young lovers feel intensely that which the mode incites them to feel. Confronted with the image of the ideal lover, each reverts to stereotype. What we have here is an existential drama of sonnet-life. The world of Romeo and Juliet, shared by Benvolio, the Montagues and Capulets, and the Prince, is a world of fixed relationships and closed assumptions. They appear as quotations, and they speak in quotations: the cliché, of which the sonnet is exemplar, is the dominant thought-form of Verona.

III

But the Petrarchan world comprehends anti-Petrarchan forces – the resistance movement, if you like. Of course an element of anti-Petrarchanism is implicit in the convention itself. An intelligent adherent to the mode is a prototype of the dandy, self-critically aware of the role he apparently acquiesces in. Such a one, perhaps, is the Romeo of the early scenes. But the resistance movement takes more overt forms than the polished oxymora that Romeo projects in I, 1. It can be observed in the Nurse, with her peasant's calculus of existence: 'I think it best you married with the County' (III, 5, 219). It is apparent in the servants' and musicians' dialogue of IV, 5, with its burlesque of grief: 'When griping grief the heart doth wound, / And doleful dumps the mind oppress . . .' (IV, 5, 123–4).[8] But the head and front of the resistance movement is Mercutio; and it is he, naming Petrarch to Romeo's face, who voices the dialectical challenge of this play:

> Now is he for the numbers that Petrarch flowed in.
> Laura to his lady was a kitchen-wench (marry, she had
> a better love to be-rhyme her), Dido a dowdy, Cleopatra
> a gypsy, Helen and Hero, hildings and harlots;
> Thisbe a grey eye or so, but not to the purpose –
> (II, 4, 38–43)

Were Mercutio in love, he would write Sonnet 130 ('My mistress' eyes are nothing like the sun').[9] As he is not, he derides his friend in what is virtually a burlesque, rhymeless sonnet:

> Romeo! Humours! Madman! Passion! Lover!
> Appear thou in the likeness of a sigh;
> Speak but one rhyme and I am satisfied!
> Cry but 'Ay me!' pronounce but love and dove . . .
> (II, 1, 7–21)

'Speak but one rhyme' implies a verdict, not only on Romeo, but on virtually everyone else in the play. Mercutio himself has a profound contempt for rhyme; he can scarcely bring himself to perpetrate a single one. His mode is a supple, virile prose, or a liberated blank verse; but preferably prose. The Queen Mab speech, as I take it, essentially validates and enlarges Mercutio. We cannot thereafter view him as a simple scoffer. His language is more *admirable* than Romeo's; it is a permanent judgement, coded into his aversion from rhyme and his mastery of the two major media. It is in prose that he presents, in a single speech, the issues, by which he demands to be judged:

> Why, is not this better now than groaning for love? Now art thou sociable, now are thou Romeo; now art thou what thou art, by art as well as nature, for this drivelling love is like a great natural that runs lolling up and down to hide his bauble in a hole.
> (II, 4, 83–7)

The pun on 'art' directs us, via the art-nature opposition, to the issues of identity and role-playing that Mercutio detects in Romeo. The nature/natural gibe is a very serious critique of Romeo, and of what he terms love. But the point, and problem of the speech lies in the intensity of the anti-Petrarchan charge. 'Bawdy' is inadequate to describe the primitive force of this image, this sexual gargoyle. It is a grimace directed at the centre of the play; and even a strong-stomached modern critic may find it too much.[10] The gravest critical error concerning *Romeo and Juliet* is to assume that the play, more or less, identifies itself with the lovers; and the violence of Mercutio's commentary is on record to remind us of the counterforce whereby the ultimate poise is achieved.

In all this, Mercutio is an extended reflection of the play's cultural context – 'topicality' is too limited and misleading a term. I am thinking of the wave of satirists who came in with the late 1590s – Hall, Marston, Donne. 'Dante and Petrarch go rudely through the door, with four centuries of European tradition. All that deifying of women amounts to nothing more than a self-deception, a projection of unsatisfied desire.'[11] Here A. J. Smith is writing of Donne, but the second sentence describes perfectly well the point that Mercutio is making to Romeo. I am not, of course, suggesting a crude reading of *Romeo and Juliet* that makes it a kind of debate between Spenser and Donne. I think rather that the dating of *Romeo and Juliet*, at the cross-roads of the 1590s, gave Shakespeare an opportunity to characterise the intellectual life of the period. It is an era of very rapid transition, and *Romeo and Juliet* assimilates and dramatises its conflicts. We can be certain that before the satirists of the fin-de-siècle had their public say, there must have been proto-Donnes and proto-Marstons of the capital's life concerned to make the – very sound—point that the bulk of sonnetteering was affected, unreal, and absurd. The thesis of Sidney and the antithesis of Donne are both, Hegelianly, present in the synthesis of 1595. And Shakespeare has described that synthesis.

Mercutio – to return to the play – is in fine the leader of the group which includes the Nurse and the comic servants. It exists to challenge the assumptions, the style, and even the diction of the Petrarchans in the centre of the stage. There is in this principle of organisation nothing original. Shakespeare had done it before, for this same city of Verona: the pretensions of the young gentlemen are savaged by everyone from Crab (parodically) upward. What is original is the means, of singular aesthetic appeal, whereby the suppression of the anti-Petrarchan voice initiates the coming of tragedy. The realist-critic of the Petrarchan world is the agent of a reality that destroys it. Mercutio's death does not refute him, it refutes the others. Without Mercutio, the position collapses. Lacking a strong, critical and intelligent impulse, the lovers with their helpers and elders are unable to cope with the demands of the new situation. The metamorphosis of Mercutio is decidedly the key to this curiously original drama.

IV

We might, I think, demonstrate the matter more elegantly by returning to the language of *Romeo and Juliet*. The central event of the play is the modulation of the realist into a governing reality. Well, but the antithesis of realism is nominalism; we might expect the first half of the play to be much engaged with the question of names. And this is in fact what we find. Of the play's thirty references to 'name', in all its forms, twenty-nine occur in the first three Acts. They are almost all associated with Romeo and Juliet, and with love. Mercutio initiates the motif parodically : 'Speak to my gossip Venus one fair word, / One nickname for her purblind son and heir, / Young Abraham Cupid . . .' (II, 1, 11–13) and continues with 'my invocation / Is fair and honest; in his mistress' name / I conjure only but to raise up him.' (II, 1, 27–9) (This is the language, if not the tone, of Sonnet 151 : 'flesh stays no farther reason, / But, rising at thy name, doth point out thee . . .') The balcony scene that follows is a sustained lyric on 'name'. The essential parts of Juliet's soliloquy are :

> O Romeo, Romeo, wherefore art thou Romeo?
> Deny thy father, and refuse thy name . . .
> 'Tis but thy name that is my enemy.
> Thou art thyself, though not a Montague.
> What's Montague? . . . O be some other name!
> What's in a name? That which we call a rose
> By any other name would smell as sweet . . .
> . . . Romeo doff thy name,
> And for thy name which is no part of thee,
> Take all myself.
>
> (II, 2, 33–49)

Romeo's self-identification is

> By a name
> I know not how to tell thee who I am.
> My name, dear saint, is hateful to myself,
> Because it is an enemy to thee.
>
> (II, 2, 53–6)

They are curiously obsessed by the relationship between names and vital essences. Juliet's 'Swear by thy gracious self, / Which is the god of my idolatry' (II, 2, 113–14) does seem to penetrate, via names, to essences; still, 'idolatry' is ominous, however consciously inflected. And Romeo, in a posture typical of the early Shakespeare's handling of young men in love, seems much more besotted with the appearance of things than his feminine counterpart. We cannot evade the ironic implications of his response to Friar Laurence's question, in the following scene:

> wast thou with Rosaline?
> *Romeo* With Rosaline, my ghostly father? No.
> I have forgot that name, and that name's woe.
> (II, 3, 44–6)

Romeo has a Caesar-like obsession with *name* as a third-person, objective entity. Note his paroxysm of grief at the news that Juliet cries on Romeo:

> As if that name,
> Shot from the deadly level of a gun,
> Did murder her; as that name's cursed hand
> Murdered her kinsman. O tell me, Friar, tell me,
> In what vile part of this anatomy
> Doth my name lodge? Tell me, that I may sack
> The hateful mansion.
> (III, 3, 102–8)

'Name', like 'rhyme', is a way of coding the apprehension of values in this society. Appearance, and form, are the realities of the Veronese. They are none the less genuine for that; but they are vulnerable. No one has the grasp of meanings apparent in 'Make but my name thy love and love that still, / And then thou lovest me, for my name is Will' (Sonnet 136).[12] This sonnet-society lacks a major sonnetteer. Not one of the three perfect sonnets has real quality, any more than the sonnet-fragments. The choric sonnets (to which one can add the Prince's final sestet) do not seek to grapple with the inwardness of the events and are, in a profound sense, the play. The only man who could write sonnets of the first order prefers to parody them; and he is dead at half-way, or perhaps at the parting of octave and sestet. But even Mercutio has the Veronese fascination with names – with Tybalt, 'Prince of Cats', the *bons* of the affected, 'villain', the fatal 'consort' (the ministrel-word) that leads to the duel. Mercutio's final 'your houses' is a reduction of the names that structure the first half of the play. 'Houses' is a variant of 'Montague' and 'Capulet', the terms that have sustained the nominalist duet of Romeo and Juliet. The last words of the play's realist are a rejection of his society's preoccupation.

V

This is a society as given to forms in grief, as in love and war. I think the most daring scene in the play IV, 5 wherein the reactions of the Capulet household to Juliet's death are detailed. Since her death is a deception, and since this scene must not duplicate the final situation, Shakespeare can permit himself a licence in characterising these people that is impossible later. Capulet's reactions are interesting. First comes the unmatchably simple and moving 'Death lies on her like an untimely frost / Upon the sweetest flower of all the field' (IV, 5, 28–9). 'Death' is perhaps as much an abstraction as a personification here : its positioning at the beginning of the line conceals, as it were, the capital. Now begins the movement to personification, to formalisation :

> Death, that hath ta'en her hence to make me wail
> Ties up my tongue and will not let me speak.
> (IV, 5, 31–2)

This is less moving. Now comes positively a conceit :

> O son, the night before thy wedding day
> Hath Death lain with thy wife. There she lies,
> Flower as she was, deflowered by him.
> Death is my son-in-law, Death is my heir . . .
> (IV, 5, 35–8)

This is, of course, dramatically compressed time, but the movement seems perfectly clear; it is from grief to mourning, from the impulse to sorrow to the outward expression of that sorrow. And the passages that follow border on the ludicrous, as Lady Capulet, Nurse, Paris, and Capulet compete with each other in an anthology of apostrophes. I do not know how these passages should be staged; but I think Shakespeare is taking advantage of a cultural fact, which is that patterns of mourning outside one's own society tend to appear faintly absurd, a suggestion normally overlaid by one's knowledge of the genuineness of the emotions. But here we are freed from the obligation to react decently, and we can admit that the Nurse's lamentation (especially) is a burlesque :

> O woe ! O woeful, woeful, woeful day !
> Most lamentable day, most woeful day
> That ever, ever I did yet behold !
> O day, O day, O day, O hateful day,

Never was seen so black a day as this.
O woeful day! O woeful day!
(IV, 5, 49–54)

The stupefying banality of this is no more than a lower-order caricature – the device is standard Shakespearean – of the gentry. And anyone in the audience who still feels that mourning, any mourning, is a serious business can safely relax during the musicians' interlude. It looks like being a good wake.

VI

The final stages of *Romeo and Juliet* are, however, the real thing, and it would be unseemly to permit the acidities of the pseudo-death scene to linger on one's tongue. The final events are essentially simple, and we should react simply to them. Nevertheless, our judgement has been carefully prepared throughout the entire play. The language of *Romeo and Juliet* is a notation that implies a judgement on its speakers, and Shakespeare exhibits, in his selection of styles, a profound detachment from the dramatis personae. Much of this detachment is, naturally, evident enough in the content of the play. I have no wish to reopen the question of the lovers' suicide – I am content with the evidence assembled by R. M. Frye that the Elizabethans would have found the suicides culpable.[13] Similarly, I accept F. M. Dickey's findings that the Elizabethans would have viewed the lovers in a much more comic light than we tend to.[14] And the play contains a clear refutation of Romeo's conduct, through Friar Laurence's rebuke in III, 3. But I want to extend this detachment to the entire dramatis personae, for it is, as I argue, at the root of the conception of tragedy here. W. H. Auden has listed ten occasions on which a character has made the wrong choice, with consequences that contribute to the ultimate fatality.[15] There is no need to weigh them here. Ten is sufficient. The point, surely, is that Verona is a wrong-choice society. It is a community fascinated with names, forms, rituals. Its citizens are passionate, impatient, intolerant, impulsive. It lacks a capacity for appraising its own values. Its Prince does not tell the community that the Montague–Capulet feud is an absurdity, he merely forbids brawling in the streets. The fatal chance of the thrust under Romeo's arm is bad luck : true. But someone would get killed in a duel, sometime; it was inevitable. Fate, then, is diffused back into the entire society. The seeds of tragedy are present even in the apparently comic world of the first two Acts – a world of young lovers and friends, comic servants and go-betweens, doddering seniors. To create a totally credible situation, which is habitually Shakespeare's objective, a much greater degree of social determinism is required than is generally understood. What we have in *Romeo and Juliet* is a complete social context for an action, a society that is unable to cope with the consequences of its own deficiencies. Even at the end, Verona has learned little. The Prince, in his epitome of the non-committal, has only

> For never was a story of more woe,
> Than this of Juliet and her Romeo.

And Montague can only make his stylised public gesture, matched by Capulet :[16]

> For I will raise her statue in pure gold,
> That whiles Verona by that *name* is known,
> There shall no figure at such rate be set
> As that of true and faithful Juliet.
> (v, 3, 299–302)

And all this is implicit from the beginning, in the characters' modes of discourse. Certainly their styles have improved – the second half of the play contains fewer rhymed couplets, more and less-stilted blank verse. But this is a relative improvement only. Their anagnorisis is as limited as the Prince's final sestet.

Closer than any other play in the canon, *Romeo and Juliet* stands near in spirit to *Love's Labour's Lost*. The Petrarchan world of Navarre, like that of Verona, is penetrated by an irrefutable and annihilating reality. And in each case the agent is a descendant of Mercury. 'Mercutio', we are told, 'is of course, mercurial; that is the humour concealed in the anagram of his name, and that is the way he behaves.'[17] Well, yes. Mercutio behaves mercurially; but so, in a different sense, does Mercade. Their relationship to the world of comedy is the same. The death of Mercutio is harsh, after the songs of Petrarch.

4 *Henry V:* The Reason Why

It is not, I take it, necessary today to argue for the double impact of *Henry V*. We can see *Henry V* as a great war play embedded in a greater anti-war play. In the theatre, the director can choose which of these two plays he intends to project, or acknowledge. So the gap between the Olivier film of 1944 and the Royal Shakespeare Company's production of the mid-sixties is enormous. But the critic can acknowledge one play only, and he is therefore committed to the larger, and necessarily ironic account of the actions recorded in Henry V. Unlike the director, he cannot, for instance, cut the conclusion of the Agincourt soliloquy: '. . . but in gross brain little wots / What watch the king keeps to maintain the peace . . .' (IV, 1, 299–300) because it might spoil the effect, if the audience actually thought about what Henry was saying. Nor can he minimise the prelates' discussion in the opening scene.[1] Broadly, the ironic reading of *Henry V*, which has received some outstandingly able advocacy,[2] seems to me unanswerable. But I shall assume at least a general acquiescence on that score, and concentrate on the mechanism of the play. It seems evident that Shakespeare's strategy is to keep his Crispin Crispian audience happy, while leaving on record the reservations that the 'other' audience can pick up. This calls for sleight-of-hand of the highest order, for the disparity between the two versions has to be indicated discreetly yet unmistakably. The relations between Chorus and play symbolise this disparity, and we can begin with them.

I

Why do we need a Chorus? This is, of course, the primary question on the mechanism of *Henry V*. Chorus himself supplies an answer: it is an apology for the 'unworthy scaffold' that is to present 'So great an object', and 'the vasty fields of France'. It was not an apology thought necessary for the battles of Tewkesbury, St Albans, Bosworth: nor, for that matter, Philippi, Actium, and Corioli. The reason seems therefore a pseudo-reason. Shakespeare is practising a sleight-of-hand, the essence of which is to induce the audience to accept the assumptions of the performance while masking the real area of operations. The Chorus, his unnecessary presence having been established, turns out to be public relations for Henry. Whatever ironic intent is in the total play, none (I think) is to be discerned in the words of Chorus. He is, as I take it, a diversionary strategy; perhaps 'over-protection' would be a better term. Imagine a production of *Henry V* shorn of the Chorus; it would be altogether a bleaker affair. We should come 'cold' to the Archbishop's plan to stave off nationalisation of Church property, and be altogether more inclined to a sceptical reception of the matter of Agincourt. As it is, our mental set is created by the glowing imagery of the Chorus. It is quite easy, in the theatre, not to take in the first (and most vital) part of the clerics' dialogue at all. The glow lingers, as it were, on the retina. The Chorus exists to bring into being, and maintain, a glamorised reading of the action. A contemporary director views him as 'an Elizabethan/High Renaissance figure speaking eloquently, confirming exciting myths and fictions for an audience: the events which are then revealed in the play are very different, more real, harder, cooler, more ambiguous.'[8] Precisely: and here the real, as distinct from nominal justification for the Chorus emerges. It is to maintain the internal balance of the total play, to redress the balance which would otherwise be heavily weighed down by the ironic possibilities in the main text. The grand image of *Henry V* is the Chorus: and that, I think, in two distinct senses. For those who recognise only the old National-Anthem-in-Five-Acts version of the play, the Chorus is simply its quintessence. He takes to the highest pitch of rhetoric the view of the action that the ordinary patriotic Englishman will take anyway. For those who prefer the main alternative (there are subdivisions, but the category is in practice perfectly plain) the Chorus is still, oddly, the play; because a disparity between Chorus and events now exists. The Chorus represents the Official Version of the events culminating in Agincourt, and the play-text contains a blend of official and unofficial versions. The Chorus is high rhetoric at long range, the play-text combines short-range rhetoric and a disturbing realism. Between the two there is incomplete identity: it is not a pronounced disjunction, but a certain crookedness, a certain lack of inevitable consequence. Just as the Chorus's reason for his own presence is not quite adequate, so his account of the action does not quite square with that amplified in the ensuing play. It is in that sense that I prefer to see the Chorus as the image of the play. He comes on stage to tell the audience the reason why; and that reason is plausible, but not quite good enough. So with the play.

II

This conception crystallises into a minute yet telling verbal circumstance. I judge the most important syntactic unit in *Henry V* to be 'therefore'. It occurs thirty-eight times (half of them from Henry), which happens to be more than in any other play in the canon.[4] The characters in this play are continually concerned, not precisely to state reasons for their actions, but to claim for their actions an inevitability flowing from their preceding reasons. There are, naturally, various ways of claiming this legitimisation of consequence. One can do it expressly or implicitly by larding one's speeches with 'God' (as Henry does habitually). Or one can follow up an image or fable with 'I this infer', as the Archbishop of Canterbury does. Or one can simply file a claim with 'So that'. Argumentation has many forms, and the verbal tic 'therefore' is merely a way of detecting them. It has been suggested that the mode of *Henry V* is the dispute.[5] There is unquestionably some substance to this – the number of disputes in *Henry V*, starting with France–England, does not admit of query – but I propose, as a more exact formulation of the idea, that the mode of *Henry V* is the dubious or fallacious argument. If the arguments so constantly advanced in *Henry V* are generally sound, then the play is a Meissonier canvas of a Great Patriotic War, Carlyle is right and Hazlitt is wrong, and modern critics have been wasting their time in peering for ironies where none exist. But if the cause be not good, then the play is an instrument for examining it. There is, after all, only one real question which it is the play's business to pose: what are the English (or British, as one begins to say at this point in the histories) doing at Agincourt? The first Act frames this question, and Michael Williams puts it. And the rest of the play is testimony relevant to a proper understanding of the question. I think, then, that the business of criticism in *Henry V* should be directed to the play's arguments. It will not be necessary to scrutinise every 'therefore', every image as argument, every appeal to God. But the modes of thought of the chief actors, as they appear in the key scenes, ought to be traced.

III

Let us try to read the early scenes: nothing, I think, is more important to an understanding of the play. Canterbury opens in the vein of political realism, itself a complete break with the Chorus. The issue is a threat to the Church. The language is terse, almost vernacular ('the scambling and unquiet times . . . 'twould drink the cup and all'), totally without pretention or affectation. This, one feels, is reality itself. As L. C. Knights remarks in a different context, 'the colloquial style is the verbal equivalent of a moral habit of seeing the naked human actuality which, in the world of political and social antagonisms, is so often obscured.'[6] But then the dialogue changes its tone.

Ely But what prevention?
Canterbury The king is full of grace and fair regard.

(One imagines a shrewd, sideways glance from Canterbury to Ely here. Ely picks up his cue, as Bishops should when Archbishops supply it.)

Ely And a true lover of the holy church.

(Your move.)
Canterbury now launches into essentially *public* oratory. 'The courses of his youth promised it not . . .' and so on, through thirty-odd lines of panegyric, punctuated only by an admiring 'We are blessed in the change' from Ely. Parts of this are notably glutinous: as

that, when he speaks,
The air, a charter'd libertine, is still,
And the mute wonder lurketh in men's ears,
To steal his sweet and honey'd sentences.
(I, 1, 47–50)

Chorus could not have put it better. The point is that this is the public address system speaking; it is a reversal of the intimate address of the scene's opening. As I read it, Canterbury (who is nobody's fool) shifts modes to indicate to his understanding subordinate what the Church's line must be. These things are not done vulgarly. Ely picks up the message:

The strawberry grows underneath the nettle
And wholesome berries thrive and ripen best
Neighbour'd by fruit of baser quality:
And so the prince obscured his contemplation
Under the veil of wildness; which, no doubt,
Grew like the summer grass, fastest by night,
Unseen, yet crescive in his faculty.
(I, 1, 60–6)

It's a dialogue of modes, Ely responding in kind with a fine instance of the image-as-sermon. Unsurprisingly, Canterbury has no wish to endure much of this; he responds with a terse two and a half lines; the way is thus open for a resumption of the non-public dialogue:

Ely But, my good lord,
How now for mitigation of this bill
Urged by the commons? Doth his majesty
Incline to it, or no?
Canterbury He seems indifferent,
Or rather swaying more upon our part
Than cherishing the exhibiters against us;
For I have made an offer to his majesty,
Upon our spiritual convocation
And in regard of causes now in hand,
Which I have open'd to his grace at large,
As touching France, to give a greater sum
Than ever at one time the clergy yet
Did to his predecessors part withal.
(I, 1, 69–81)

We have left the pulpit for the closet. I detect, then, three phases in the clerics' talk, private–public–private. The relations between these phases are not formally stated at all; it is all done by implication and style. In Shakespeare, matters tend to be explained by what comes some time after, and not immediately. It is so here, and Canterbury's syntax provides the gloss: '*For* I have made an offer . . .' So much for the 'grace and fair regard': now we know why Canterbury thought it necessary to turn the mode at this point. It would have been crude to a degree to omit the intermediary aria and proceed directly to the political manœuvre, after Ely's initial question of line 21. The prelates are acknowledging the needs of public theatre, the version of events that must be conveyed to the world to account for, and thus to expedite, Henry's regard for the Church and the actions stemming therefrom.

And theatre is, naturally, the total context of I, 2. Here there is nothing private: the stage presents a great King who is bent on war, but only in such a way that all elements in the State combine to that end, 'congreeing like music'. What he does, he will do for certain apparent reasons. All relations are dynamic: the King is being urged, but is himself ensuring that he will be so urged. Those urging him know that it is their role to urge, and that they will prevail if they discharge that function with animation. Each obstacle that the King raises will be overcome; it must be so overcome, else there will be no decision. King, lords temporal and spiritual congree like music. First comes the disclaimer of regal responsibility: the Archbishop is charged to be mindful of the consequences 'Of what your reverence shall incite us to. / Therefore take heed how you impawn our person . . .' (20–1). Then comes the Archbishop's legal justification of the claim. It poses a problem for directors; they like to make the courtiers yawn, shuffle, and so on. Justifiably : if a sector of the stage audience chooses to regard the speech as a rigmarole, this is not inapposite. It is too long to be taken seriously. This farrago of names is sad stuff, and grows steadily less convincing as it proceeds; as, surely, Shakespeare intends it to appear. The irony emerges fairly clearly in the Archbishop's clinching '*So that*, as clear as is the summer's sun . . .'(86) Few things could be less clear. But for those who have been paying attention, the irony of content is superb :

> The Archbishop's argument in support of Henry's claim to the French throne – that a claimant descended in the female line from the senior branch of a royal house takes precedence in the succession over one descended in the male line from a junior branch – in reality proves, not that Henry is the rightful King of France, but that he is not the rightful King of England. As Shakespeare himself had twice demonstrated at length in earlier plays, the house of Mortimer was descended in the female line from the third son of Edward III, through whom Henry claimed the French throne, whereas the house of Lancaster was descended in the male line from the fourth son (*1 Henry VI*, II, 5, 71–8; *2 Henry VI*, II, 2.)[7]

It all comes down to Henry's marvellously flat, open line : 'May I with right and conscience make this claim?' (96) It is useless to talk of the meaning of this line : the meaning is in the inflection that the actor gives it, and all we can know is that Henry, at that moment, finds it necessary to pose a clear question. He gets a clear evasion :

> *Canterbury* The sin upon my head, dread sovereign!
> For in the book of Numbers is it writ,
> When the man dies, let the inheritance
> Descend unto the daughter. Gracious lord,
> Stand for your own; unwind your bloody flag . . .[8]
> (97–101)

Ely, Exeter, Westmoreland, and Canterbury now throng around the King, presenting a glamorised and impassioned poster of the war. It is completed, with deep sense of timing, by Canterbury :

> O, let their bodies follow, my dear liege,
> With blood and sword and fire to win your right;

In aid whereof we of the spiritualty
Will raise your highness such a mighty sum
As never did the clergy at one time
Bring in to any of your ancestors.

(130–5)

The offer of the subsidy is now public. It directly follows *right*, and 'in aid thereof' states a seemingly logical, in context unchallengeable, connection between *war*, *right*, *subsidy*. The crux of the argument is over, and Henry now raises questions of ways and means. The Scots? There are defences against the Scots. Images supply the argument here: England is an 'eagle', Scotland a 'weasel', though the respective activities of the Scots and English seem not dissimilar. The rhetoric begs its own questions. Exeter's idea of a balanced offensive-defensive posture gives the Archbishop the opportunity for his sermon:

Therefore doth heaven divide
The state of man in divers functions,
Setting endeavour in continual motion;
To which is fixed, as an aim or butt,
Obedience: *for* so work the honey-bees,
Creatures that by a rule in Nature teach
The act of order to a peopled kingdom.
They have a king and officers of sorts;
Where some, like magistrates, correct at home,
Others, like merchants, venture trade abroad,
Others, like soldiers, armed in their stings,
Make boot upon the summer's velvet buds,
Which pillage they with merry march bring home
To the tent-royal of their emperor . . .

(183–96)

We really have to pause to take in the effrontery of this speech. Its central analogy ('my metaphor was drawn from bees', as Canon Chasuble said) is in truth a non-analogy, as presented here. Bees, apparently, have something to teach the king, officers, merchants, etc., of human society, in that they have a kind of king, officers, and merchants, which resemble king, officers, and merchants. How can they 'teach the act of order', or anything else, to a 'peopled kingdom' when what they display is identified in purely reflective categories? The staggering tautology of all this is a fully-orchestrated amplification of Ely's earlier discovery that grass grows, 'crescive'. What, then, is the point (tone, as in 'merry march', aside)? Canterbury, after holding up this mirror to a Christian king, now moves to a different plane of logic:

I this infer,
That many things, having full reference
To one consent, may work contrariously:
As many arrows, loosed several ways,
Come to one mark; as many ways meet in one town;
As many fresh streams meet in one salt sea;
As many lines close in the dial's centre;
So may a thousand actions, once afoot,
End in one purpose, and be all well borne
Without defeat.

(204–13)

The happy ambiguity of 'so', which can suggest a consequence as well as a comparison, is resourcefully exploited by the Archbishop. By a process of thought, which it would defame the human intellect to dignify by any other term than 'association', Canterbury has moved from the beehive to France, and victoriously too. The keystone of this triumph of logic is now lowered in: '*Therefore* to France, my lord . . .' (213). I find it impossible to believe that an intelligent, educated member of Shakespeare's audience, who would have received approximately a hundred times the training in logic and rhetoric that his average modern counterpart has had, would have been taken in by this parcel of non-sequiturs. It is rhetoric designed to embellish a predetermined policy, and identifiable as fustian. The Elizabethan audience, after all, was a good deal more alert to the dangers of argument by fable than we are. Here, for instance, is Wilson on the value of fables:

> The feined Fables, such as are attributed unto brute beastes . . . not onely . . . delite the rude and ignorant, but also they helpe much for perswasion . . . because such as speake in open audience have ever mo fooles to heare them, then wisemen to give judgment . . . The multitude (as Horace doth say) is a beast . . . use the quiddities of *Dunce*, to set forth Gods misteries: and you shall see the ignorant (I warrant you) either fall a sleepe, or els bid you farewell. The multitude must needes be made merrie: . . . The Romaine *Menenius Agrippa*, alledging upon a time, a Fable of the conflict made betwixt the parts of a mans bodie, and his bellie: quieted . . . the uprore of sedicious Rebelles . . .[9]

Wilson, be it noted, is less impressed by the fable of the belly than modern commentators on *Coriolanus*. I think that a sector of the original audience to *Henry V* might have been correspondingly more resistant to the sophistical allurements of the bees.

The tennis ball incident now supervenes. Since the King has already determined to invade France ('Now are we well resolved', 222) the Dauphin's insult is simply a post hoc opportunity for more political theatre. Nothing that Henry says to the Ambassadors indicates that the decision has already been taken. The only conclusion that the French could draw from the outburst is that the Dauphin has pushed Henry over the edge of decision. The final couplet is a clear statement that the responsibility is the Dauphin's:

> and tell the Dauphin,
> His jest will savour but of shallow wit,
> When thousands weep more than did laugh at it.
> (294–6)

That is the 'reason', an elaborated 'therefore'. The final scene of this political theatre is a dramatisation of false logic.

There remains the King's admonition to the Court. It is a revealing sampling of Henry's mannerisms of speech and thought:

> *Exeter* This was a merry message.
> *K. Henry* We hope to make the sender blush at it.
> *Therefore*, my lords, omit no happy hour
> That may give furtherance to our expedition;
> For we have now no thought in us but France,
> Save those to God, that run before our business.
> *Therefore* let our proportions for these wars
> Be soon collected and all things thought upon
> That may with reasonable swiftness add
> More feathers to our wings; for, God before,
> We'll chide this Dauphin at his father's door.
> *Therefore* let every man now task his thought,
> That this fair action may on foot be brought.
> (309–10)

Note the patterning of key words: Therefore/God/therefore/God/therefore. Draw, one might say, your own conclusions: the message Henry signals is disarmingly clear. It is essentially the message contained in his peroration to Scroop:

> I will weep for thee;
> For this revolt of thine, methinks, is like
> Another fall of man.
> (II, 2, 140–2)

Henry's commands realise a divine logic: he is the chosen instrument of God, whom to revolt against were to defy Him.

IV

In all this, I doubt if the issue of 'sincerity' can usefully be raised. Henry is an efficient political animal; all that he does is directed towards an end. Political man 'is the role', 'the person is the function', as Alvin Kernan indicates.[10] The King has a natural understanding of 'verita effettuale', in Machiavelli's phrase. Take the speech before Harfleur. It is a further instance of Henry's talent for presenting a form of reasoning that suits his purposes, and for shifting the responsibility for unpleasant events elsewhere : 'you yourselves are cause'. But it works. Harfleur falls, there is no sack. There can be no great complaint against Henry here : but note the mental process :

> This is the latest parle we will admit :
> *Therefore* to our best mercy give yourselves ;
> Or like to men proud of destruction
> Defy us to our worst . . .
>
> (III, 3, 2–6)

The conclusions are derived, with a show of logic, from what is actually a prior decision and an act of will, not an objective reality : 'This is the latest parle we will admit.' After the account of the English soldiers following an assault (which bears little resemblance to the stainless warriors pictured in the Agincourt speech) Henry concludes

> *Therefore*, you men of Harfleur,
> Take pity of your town and of your people,
> Whiles yet my soldiers are in my command ;
>
> (III, 3, 27–9)

Henry's talent for divesting himself of responsibility (though not power) at convenient phases of a sustained operation amounts to genius. Granted, this is precisely what the immediate Harfleur operation demands, and which military usage sanctioned. But the underlying mental process is too shrewdly self-serving, too much in line with the earlier sampling of Henry's mind for us to accord it much more than the respect due to a professional of political life.

Agincourt is the test. Everything that precedes it is public, and subject to the judgement that public figures are obliged to act in ways that are not comparable with those of private men.[11] In IV, 1, the private world of a public man is examined. It is the only scene in which this is done, and the most important in the play. The interrogation, conducted with a masterly intimacy through the humble figures of

Bates and Williams, enforces upon the King the inescapable consequences of a public act. He has, at last to defend himself, and not simply to charge Archbishops, admonish conspirators, and threaten besieged towns. He does it badly. The passage has often been analysed,[12] and I need only point to its salient features. Williams's speculation on the heavy reckoning that the King must make if the cause is bad is no more than Henry himself had said to the Archbishop. Goddard phrases the charge precisely: 'The King was willing to put the responsibility on an archbishop but he is unwilling to let his soldiers put the responsibility on a king.'[13] Henry's response is a long, an over-long inflation of the initial and subtly evasive 'So'. The essence of it is that he shifts the emphasis from *King* to *subject*. The clinching 'therefore' ushers in the injunction to the soldier to look to his own duty, followed with complete predictability by the association of duty with Gods' will:

> *Therefore* should every soldier in the wars do as every sick man in his bed, wash every mote out of his conscience: and dying so, death is to him advantage; or not dying, the time was blessedly lost wherein such preparation was gained: and in him that escapes, it were not sin to think that, making God so free an offer, He let him outlive that day to see His greatness and to teach others how they should prepare.
>
> (IV, 1, 189–96)

Overall, it is not a convincing answer ('What a poor, muddled, and irrelevant answer it is', says Palmer),[14] but it can just be defended on the grounds that the King has a military duty to make the soldier feel the weight of the moral harness on his back. This is still the public man, with duties to perform that transcend attention to the niceties of argument. But the soliloquy that follows gives it all away. 'Upon the king . . .' and there follows a classic statement of the office-holder's revulsion against office. Here again the drift of the complaint is humanly acceptable, if scarcely impressive. It is an established fact that office-holders are disposed to live with their burdens. But the conclusion is insufferable. 'He sighs to think that the gross brain of the peasant little wots what watch the king keeps *to maintain the peace* and within a few hours he is to win a famous victory in a war of conquest.'[15] Unless one allows that 'peace' (domestic, in England) is maintainable only through external aggression, the conclusion stares down Irony itself. And here Henry's secret emerges. Like other successful politicians, he is, simply, not very interesting. No more than Coriolanus' do his soliloquies stand examination.[16] His mental and physical constitution is a mechanism for producing political results, not self-awareness. Henry is devious without being complicated (rather like the play). A man who could utter 'peace', in that context, to himself, and go on to pray for forgiveness for his father's fault in compassing the crown, falls something short of intellectual adequacy. He is not, perhaps a hypocrite: but then hypocrisy is a severely taxing term to define. Let us say instead that Henry has a low threshold of self-deception.

Henry's mental set is the inner play of *Henry V*. It corresponds with the outer structure of *Henry V*, an instinctual reaching after success with a capacity to evade intellectually the issues involved. What Henry knows is what it is necessary to know, with the addition of 'therefore' before and 'God' after. As practical logic, it passes muster in this world. It even passes the test of courtship in Act v: 'Come, your answer in broken music; for thy voice is music and thy English broken; *therefore*, queen of all, Katherine, break thy mind to me in broken English; wilt thou have me?' (v, 2, 263–6). The context is relatively trivial, but it is a final instance of Henry's trick of insinuating apparent consequence in all that he wishes or does. He submits to the will of the universe; he will always be the beneficiary of Providence's favours, since what he receives will be attributed to divine blessing. Such a man is, in this world, invincible; and the French King, who is best placed to pass judgment on him, has this perception: 'Yes, my lord, you see them perspectively, the cities turned into a maid . . .' (v, 2, 348–9). Equally, in the maid he discerns the cities. With this kind of bifocal vision, nothing is impossible, not even love. There is in Henry's final line a sublime assurance, the mental invulnerability of the man who will always be able to live with himself: 'And may our oaths well kept and prosperous be!' We can be sure that the ultimate responsibility for keeping or breaking the oaths will always be with the French. Whoever may be guilty of *mauvaise foi*, it will not be Henry.

Henry V is a statement of a willed success that overbears the reservations, doubt and criticisms expressed in the text. The conclusions, which follow the fiercely iterated *therefores*, tend to legitimise retroactively the premises. But this they cannot quite do; and we end the record of a supreme triumph with the knowledge that Henry V will be followed by Henry VI, that the cycle of history will move to an unparalleled disaster already chronicled by Shakespeare. The final doubt, which it falls to Chorus to concede, is that of History.

To call Henry 'Shakespeare's ideal King' is a satire upon ideals. He is merely successful, and one need go no further. Perhaps, in a larger sense, it is indeed a history of the nation that Shakespeare is writing. One does not turn for dramatic criticism to Churchill. But his account of the preliminaries to the Agincourt campaign is, in its way, a first-class gloss on Shakespeare's play, and much superior in understanding to most of the criticism of *Henry V*:

> Council and Parliament alike showed themselves suddenly bent on war with France. As was even then usual in England, they wrapped this up in phrases of opposite import. The lords knew well, they said, 'that the King will attempt nothing that is not to the glory of God, and will eschew the shedding of Christian blood; if he goes to war the cause will be the renewal of his rights, not his own wilfulness.' Bishop Beaufort opened the session of 1414 with a sermon upon 'Strive for the truth unto death' and the exhortation 'While we have time, let us do good to all men.' This was understood to mean the speedy invasion of France.[17]

5 'To say one': An Essay on *Hamlet*

The beginning of Act v, Scene 2 finds Hamlet in a trough between action, released for once from the immediate stimuli of events. He is merely discussing his affairs with Horatio. It is a still moment, not with the felt danger of the moment that follows the acceptance of Laertes' challenge, but freer, less constrained. Horatio reminds him gently that the English authorities must shortly report on the death of Rosencrantz and Guildenstern. And Hamlet responds with these words:

> It will be short,
> The *interim's* mine, and a mans life's no more
> Then to say one.

That is what we have, and I reproduce it exactly in the terms that the Folio, our sole authority for this passage, supplies. *A mans life's no more then to say one*. What does it mean? The editors – with, I think, a single major exception – pass the line by, its meaning being so obvious as to warrant no commentary. But I find that to explain the line, if I can, requires me to explain the play.

An editor can look the other way, but a translator cannot. We can glance at two distinguished translations. Schlegel appears to stonewall successfully with 'Ein Menschenleben ist als zählt man eins' : in fact he has given the phrase a decisive inclination, for 'zählen' is to count, not utter. André Gide makes this rendering even clearer : 'Et la vie d'un homme ne laisse même pas compter jusqu'à deux.' Since the tendency of French is always to be reductive of meanings, and of Shakespeare to expand possibilities, we can start with Gide's – single – meaning. He takes Hamlet to be saying that man's life is brief, and that one must be ready for action. That is a legitimate meaning. John Dover Wilson suggests, in his New Cambridge edition, that 'one' is the fencer's word, the exclamation that one utters at the climax of the lunge : 'a single pass, then will finish Claudius off'.[1] I think he must be right, but here too the single meaning pauperises the riches of Shakespeare's word-play here. 'One' is of all numbers the most resonant. It bears the implications of unity and self-hood, and it has moreover a significant past in *Hamlet*. Is not Hamlet saying that man's life is a quest for unity, for the oneness of self and situation? And is not the final scene the statement of a profound accord between self and situation, action and awareness?

But let us explore some of the ways in which the final scene does, in truth, permit Hamlet to say 'one'.

I

Hamlet is not a play that admits of ready, or final, description. I find L. C. Knight's term 'the Hamlet consciousness'[2] helpful, and I prefer to think of the play as a prolonged description of a single consciousness. At the beginning, that consciousness is aligned against its situation. It rejects external events, it lacks a stable base of self-hood: it is profoundly disturbed. At the end of the play, the consciousness is fully aligned with its situation. It is sufficiently self-aware, it has a base for judgement and action. Hamlet is, so to speak, *comfortable*. That, in broadest outline, is what happens in *Hamlet*.

Certain elements predominate in the Hamlet consciousness, and can be identified here. We might, I think, begin by discarding a misleading term that figures in the commentaries, 'intellectual'. Hamlet is not an intellectual, in the sense that he is given to rational analysis of a problem. The formulation of categories and issues is not his forte. He has a superb, intuitive intelligence, but that is something quite different. This type of mind is especially good at perceiving meanings reflected back from the environment. A flair for symbolism is central to a poet, dangerous (if still vital) to a thinker. I instance the Danish drinking practices, the player's emotion, Fortinbras's march to Poland: events supply their meaning for Hamlet. But they have meaning only to the receiving mind, and to find 'sermons in stones' has always a certain intellectual *naïveté*. (There is no such thing as a symbol *per se*.) The crucial sampling of Hamlet's powers as intellectual is the 'To be or not to be' soliloquy. It is unreasonable to treat it as a philosophical disquisition – it is an associative meditation, the mind reviewing a diorama of concepts and images. But it is fair to point out that it suggests, in outline, a logical structure. Harry Levin, indeed, has stressed that Hamlet is using 'the method preferred by Renaissance logicians . . . the dichotomy, which chopped its subjects down by dividing them in half, and subdividing the resultant divisions into halves again.'[3] Nevertheless, there are so many questions left hanging in the air that the soliloquy appears to me quite unlogical in essence, if not in form. I instance a few: 'To be, or not to be: that is the question' surely implies another question. This is true whether (*a*) one accents *that*, implying the rejection of a preceding question (*b*) one accents *is*, reaffirming the proposition after a previous doubt (*c*) renders *that is* as a spondee, thus more subtly reaffirming the question after a doubt. Then, is 'in the mind' a tautology ('nobler' is a mental quality) or a meaningful choice, 'suffering' to occur to the body or the mind? Does 'And by opposing end them' mean that the forces of outrageous Fortune can be physically defeated, or that the act of opposition in itself is a means of dispersing them, or that the act of opposition must mean death, with its own resolution of the problem? Again, 'puzzles the will': this I take to be a fusion of 'puzzles the mind' and 'inhibits the will'. Is Hamlet aware of this fusion, or confusion? Presumably not, since he arrives at 'Thus conscience does make cowards of us all; / And thus . . .' as though a logical terminus of argument had been arrived at. He is, like his twin Brutus, a poor reasoner – just as Brutus begins with his conclusion ('It must be by his death') and then goes on to discover reasons, Hamlet begins with the reasoning, and then – more subtly – ends with what looks like a conclusion but is in fact the unacknowledged premise of the meditation. A good argument may be circular, as may a bad: the line of Hamlet's argument is not known to geometry. Whatever else Hamlet is, he is not an intellectual.[4]

The foundation of the play is precisely this separation between premise and conclusion, between action and awareness. This remains true even though the acknowledged premises—belief in ghosts, questions of damnation, conscience, and so on – may be, objectively, perfectly sound. The play is not concerned to identify the sources of this disjunction: it states the fact. And it presents a final situation in which the disjunction has either ceased to exist, or ceased to be important. Until then, Hamlet has at times appeared uncommonly reminiscent of Nietzsche's idealist: 'The creature who has reasons for remaining in the dark about himself, and is clever enough to remain in the dark about these reasons.'

II

The Hamlet consciousness is strongly egocentric, with an impulse to self-protection that takes several forms. A vein of self-vindication, which is a part of self-affirmation, runs throughout the play. The occasions on which Hamlet blames himself are obvious enough. Not so well understood are the passages in which Hamlet is providing a kind of alibi for himself. His opening words (after a muttered aside) negative the King, placing Claudius in the wrong; and his first speech of any length is a sustained justification of his appearance and conduct to the Queen, and Court:

> Seems, madam! nay, it is; I know not 'seems'.
> . . . these indeed seem,
> For they are actions that a man might play:
> But I have that within which passeth show;
> These but the trappings and the suits of woe.
> (I, 2, 76–86)

There is here not only a defence, but an implicit appeal to the verdict of the Court. Then, in his discourse to Horatio and Marcellus on the sentry-platform, comes:

> So, oft it chances in particular men,
> That for some vicious mole of nature in them,
> As, in their birth – *wherein they are not guilty,*
> *Since nature cannot choose his origin* –

A man is guiltless of his genetic heritage: but note the conclusion:

> Shall in the *general censure* take corruption
> From that particular fault:
> (I, 4, 23–36)

A curious word, *censure,* and a curious conclusion. Hamlet does not say that mankind is, of its origins, condemned to err or sin. He says that *public opinion* will regard the man as stained by the single fault. And that consideration troubles him. (The final word in the speech, 'scandal', drives home the point.) *Censure,* moreover, is a word that reaches out, for Hamlet uses it later of an audience ('the censure of the which one must in your allowance o'erweigh a whole theatre of others', III, 2, 31–3). Is there not a strong hint here of what is plain elsewhere, that a part of Hamlet's self is derived from the opinion of others, that is to say, his audience, and that he is aware of this?

The existence of this audience is vital to the elucidation of 'That would be scann'd' (III, 3, 75). There is a problem here, and the editors have closed their ranks around it. All modern editions which I have consulted punctuate this passage with a colon or period after 'scann'd' and the universal gloss is that 'would be' here means 'requires to be'. 'Scann'd,' is given as 'scrutinised', and the statement is thus rendered 'That needs to be scrutinised / considered carefully.' I propose an entirely different reading here. 'Scan', in the fourth sense listed by the

OED, means 'to interpret, assign a meaning to'. If we accept this, 'would be' takes on its normal modern conditional meaning. The reading looks stronger if we refer back to the pointing of the Second Quarto and the Folio, so often superior to modern punctuation. The Second Quarto gives no punctuation at all after 'scann'd':

> Now might I doe it, but now a is a praying,
> And now Ile doo't, and so a goes to heaven,
> And so am I revendge, that would be scand
> A villaine kills my father, and for that,
> I his sole sonne, doe this same villaine send
> To heaven.

The Folio gives a comma, thus:

> Now might I do it pat, now he is praying,
> And now Ile doo't, and so he goes to Heaven,
> And so am I reveng'd: that would be scann'd,
> A Villaine killes my Father, and for that
> I his soule Sonne, do this same Villaine send
> To heaven.

This rapid, fluent pointing makes the syntax and meaning perfectly clear. 'A Villaine kills my Father' is now a noun clause subordinate to 'scann'd', and not an autonomous unit of thought. I claim no originality for this reading: the *OED* actually cites the above passage in support of its fourth sense. (It cites other, contemporary passages for this sense.) But we have to conduct this exercise to jettison a useless (and in my view, erroneous) meaning that has established itself over the years. For 'that would be scann'd' now means: 'that is how public opinion would interpret the matter', and the centre of the play shifts slightly but unmistakably. Hamlet's conscience increasingly takes on the aspect of the approval conferred on the self by others.

Allied to this consideration are Hamlet's uses of the 'antic disposition'. He exploits it with a certain elemental calculation. He indeed, with a certain premonitory awareness of the possibilities of madness, introduces the subject to his immediate audience: 'As I perchance hereafter *shall think meet* / To put an antic disposition on:' (I, 5, 171–2). And this disguise has notable defensive qualities, throughout the manœuvring of Acts II and III. At the same time, it takes on a therapeutic function. 'In personating a mad Hamlet, Hamlet is in fact personating a chaos of his inner self. It both is and is not Hamlet.'[5] But Hamlet is perfectly capable of distancing himself from his madness, when it suits him. 'Lay not that flattering unction to your soul, / That not your trespass, but my madness speaks' he tells Gertrude (III, 4, 144–5). To Laertes, before the Court, he proclaims :

> This presence knows,
> And you must needs have heard, how I am punish'd
> With sore distraction. What I have done,
> That might your nature, honour and exception
> Roughly awake, I here proclaim was madness.
> Was't Hamlet wrong'd Laertes? Never Hamlet :
> If Hamlet from himself be ta'en away,
> And when he's not himself does wrong Laertes,
> Then Hamlet does it not, Hamlet denies it.
> Who does it, then? His madness :
>
> (v, 2, 239–48)

This speech is normally taken as a handsome, indeed noble offer of amends. On the contrary, I regard it as an adroit and (largely successful) attempt to win over public opinion, and to place the responsibility for his actions on to his 'distraction'. It is disingenuous to plead the 'antic disposition' which he himself chose. The speech is an *apologia pro vita sua,* disguised as an apology. If this reading seems too harsh, I ask for an explanation of 'I'll be your foil, Laertes : in mine ignorance / Your skill shall, like a star i' th' darkest night, / Stick fiery off indeed.' (v, 2, 266–8) Hamlet knows perfectly well, and has told Horatio earlier, that he is in excellent training and will win at the odds. He is in fact, exhibiting a widely-encountered trait, that of the player who cries down his skill either to lull his opponent or to magnify his achievement. We should today call it gamesmanship : we should certainly not sentimentalise Hamlet's conduct. Hamlet – and here we move to the existential truth of the situation – is presenting himself to the Court as the flower of Renaissance chivalry, an illustration stepped forth from the pages of Castiglione, the fencer whose success comes always as a surprise to himself. Besides, the Queen has let him know, through a messenger, that some kind of graceful gesture ('some gentle entertainment to Laertes') would be in order. And he now divests himself of his responsibility for outrageous conduct. He is then, starring in the drama about to be played. And the drama ends, for Hamlet, with his concern for his 'wounded name', i.e. his reputation.

I am suggesting, then, that Hamlet's consciousness exhibits a profound concern for himself, for his *self*. This is far more than a simple concern to protect his body, though it includes that consideration. It is rather a consistent desire to present his actions in the most favourable light, an awareness that the 'censure of the judicious' is what matters. Horatio is several things for Hamlet : a friend and aide, a sounding-board, an instrument for communication with the world, a participant in the self-dialogue. It is to himself, as well as to Horatio, that Hamlet says 'is't not perfect conscience, / To quit him with this arm?' (v, 2, 67–8) Hamlet needs the approval of himself and of others. He does not get it in the passage I have just cited, for Horatio turns the subject instead of answering directly. But it is with others that the final appeal lies, and to others that the consciousness of this supreme egotist is directed.

III

And this is contained within the final element in Hamlet's consciousness that I wish to touch on, his awareness of self as that of the actor. Maynard Mack is surely right in taking ' "Act" . . . to be the play's radical metaphor . . . What, this play asks again and again, is an act? What is its relation to the inner act, the intent?'[6] Michael Goldman has also written well of the play as a search for the significance of action.[7] I want here, however, merely to stress the psychological implications of 'actor' for Hamlet.

An actor, as Mr. Goldman observes, is a man who wants to play Hamlet.[8] Hamlet, I would continue, is an actor profoundly dissatisfied with his part, now that he has got it. His opening scene (I, 2) is consistent with this view. It is one of the classical paradoxes of theatre: *Flourish. Enter Claudius King of Denmark, Gertrude, the Queen: Council, as Polonius, and his son, Laertes, Hamlet and others.* An impressive entrance: but no audience has ever looked at Claudius, or ever will. It is looking at the still, aloof figure who alone of the Court has not abandoned mourning, and is effortlessly accomplishing that most exquisite of actor's satisfactions, wordlessly upstaging a whole cast. In context, indeed, he is destroying the production, Claudius' first speech from the Throne. But that is not how it appears to Hamlet. *He* is upstaged by Claudius. We must remember how Hamlet reacts to bad acting – the directive to the players, the explosion at Ophelia's funeral, 'Nay, an thou'lt mouth, / I'll rant as well as thou' (v, 1, 306–7) followed by the later admission 'But, sure, the bravery of his grief did put me / Into a towering passion.' (v, 2, 79–80) And in his opening scene Claudius is *bad*, as he never is again. His speech is a series of contorted subordinate clauses, collapsing into main clauses that themselves crumple into further subordinates. Claudius is, of course, nervous – the jumpy, slightly illogical transitions give him away. ('now follows . . . So much for him. / Now for ourself . . .' Claudius has earlier talked of himself; in fact he goes on to talk of further action in the Fortinbras affair, a matter he has just seemed to dismiss.) Claudius gives the impression of continually backing into meaning, a process which continues until 'But now, my cousin Hamlet, and my son' (I, 2, 64). I labour the point, which is made vastly more subtly in the text, that Claudius is not doing too well in I, 2. And this is the man who has dispossessed Hamlet. May we not add, to the ferment of emotions expressed in the first soliloquy, an inchoate rage that this far from well-graced figure has annexed *his* role?

We may, of course, reject the possibility, on the grounds that the first soliloquy can only express what is there. In this most devious of all plays, that is scarcely an adequate position; for we have then to explain away Hamlet's later, and perfectly unequivocal statement to Horatio, that Claudius 'Popp'd in between the election and my hopes' (V, 2, 65). There are really only two ways of taking this reference, which is presumably a crystallisation of the earlier 'Excitements of my reason and my blood' (IV, 4, 58). Either Hamlet is providing a pseudo-motive, a rounding-out of the indictment against Claudius to make it respectable to Horatio and himself : or a genuine motive, slowly rising from the depths of his mind, has now broken surface and can be formulated and uttered. I take the second possibility to be the right one. Hamlet, then, is enmeshed in a central paradox. His role requires him to 'act' – to feign, put on an antic disposition, to produce and introduce a play, to assume different styles of speech, to plot and deceive – and moreover to *act*, to resolve the whole Claudius problem : yet the role is the wrong one for him. And what, then, is the right role? It is the function of the play to answer that question.

IV

The features of the Hamlet consciousness, then, I take to be these : an intuitive though not wholly rational intelligence, an egocentricity that is especially concerned with the protection of his self as it appears to others, and an actor's capacity to appreciate that self in its manœuvrings. The course of the play demonstrates, I suggest, the truth of what that 'strange fellow' whom Ulysses has been reading has to say :

> Who, in his circumstance, expressly proves
> That no man is the lord of anything,
> Though in and of him there be much consisting,
> Till he communicate his parts to others;
> Nor doth he of himself know them for aught
> Till he behold them form'd in the applause
> Where they're extended :
>
> (*Troilus and Cressida*, III, 3, 114–20)

'Applause' : that is a part of the resolution of the *Hamlet* issues. Now : my central contention is that Hamlet is a man moving towards the final awareness and affirmation of self. We must, therefore, regard the death of Hamlet as his final statement, and while it is tedious to work backwards from it – progressive chronology has too many uses to be lightly discarded – I think we ought to take note of the quality of that final position. Hamlet's death is curiously gratuitous, actorish. All the other deaths (of the protagonists) in Shakespeare's major tragedies have an elemental, obvious necessariness. A continued living (*pace* Johnson) is unthinkable for Lear, as for Othello, Macbeth, Coriolanus, and Antony. There is, simply, nothing to add to their lives. But Hamlet has, as it seems, much to live for. He is young, greatly gifted, likely to have proved most royal. His death is unfortunate and premature. It certainly appears to be of a different order from the other major tragic figures. But is it? I prefer to advance the hypothesis of the necessary death, that is, the completed life-statement. I regard the final position as the consummation (Hamlet's own word) of his life, one that combines the notions of significant and expressive action, duties accomplished, and the assurance that the 'mutes or audience' will be given the full information necessary for the understanding and appreciation of the spectacle they have just witnessed. This latter is the only point that seems to concern Hamlet at the last. He raises the matter, and elaborates it after Horatio's impulsive gesture of suicide. The Court/audience must applaud, and approve. The death scene of Hamlet is, then, satisfying in a double sense. Hamlet the actor, and the actor playing Hamlet, fuse in the climax of the drama.

V

That is the situation at the moment of Hamlet's death. We can now read more closely the movement leading up to it, that is to say the final scene (v, 2). Since Hamlet's drive towards significant action takes the mode of the duellist and fighter, we can note that the metaphor of fighting virtually opens the scene. There is much imagery of war throughout the play, now much better understood than it used to be;[9] the point of Hamlet's metaphor here is that it reflects a change of mental orientation :

> Sir, in my heart there was a kind of fighting,
> That would not let me sleep :
>
> (v, 2, 4–5)

'Sleep' : the threat to sleep, in the 'To be or not to be' soliloquy, and the admission to Rosencrantz and Guildenstern (II, 2, 262) is bad dreams. Now it is 'a kind of fighting'. That is action, and aggressive action. Hamlet goes on to tell the story. He tells it well, with a relish of its dramatic possibilities and his own role:

> Being thus be-netted round with villainies, –
> Ere I could make a prologue to my brains,
> They had begun the play –
> (v, 2, 29–31)

This is an obvious and characteristic concept of the self as hero. Less obvious is the import of his action: he imitates Claudius, he becomes Claudius in his pastiche of the King's tumid rhetoric:

> As England was his faithful tributary,
> As love between them like the palm might flourish,
> As peace should still her wheaten garland wear
> And stand a comma 'tween their amities,
> And many such-like 'As'es of great charge.
> (v, 2, 39–43)

(The style of this missive is assimilated into his later note to Claudius, details of which we have already been given (IV, 7, 43–8). It is florid, politic, dangerous. Hamlet is taking on the persona, or the assumptions, of Claudius.) And, in a moment of exquisite symbolism, he ratifies his action with his father's seal:

> I had my father's signet in my purse,
> Which was the model of that Danish seal:
> (v, 2, 49–50)

Hamlet now becomes Hamlet senior. Is it possible that Hamlet, with his flair for symbolic interpretation, has no inkling of what he is doing? The central fact is clear: Hamlet is now moving towards the mode of his father, as politician, fighter, and – the encounter with Fortinbras comes to mind – as duellist. This is the vital metaphor, the self-conceptualisation that Hamlet projects:

> Why, man, they did make love to this employment;
> They are not near my conscience; their defeat
> Does by their own insinuation grow:
> 'Tis dangerous when the baser nature comes
> Between the pass and fell incensed points
> Of mighty opposites.
> (v, 2, 57–62)

In the immediate context, this is a further piece of self-justification; the point is that it is dangerous to come between two duellists, and thus Hamlet acquits himself of any guilt in the deaths of Rosencrantz and Guildenstern. But the justification pushes Hamlet a little more firmly in the direction in which he is moving anyway. To be guiltless, he must be a duellist. Horatio's exclamation, 'Why, what a king is this!' leads Hamlet to his vindication of his future conduct:

> Does it not, thinks't thee, stand me now upon –
> He that hath kill'd my king and whored my mother,
> Popp'd in between the election and my hopes,
> Thrown out his angle for my proper life,
> And with such cozenage – is't not perfect conscience,
> To quit him with this arm? and is't not to be damn'd,
> To let this canker of our nature come
> In further evil?
>
> (v, 2, 63–70)

That is the bill of indictment against Claudius, and it is the basis of the appeal to Horatio's sense of 'conscience', as to Hamlet's own. It is, even its final image, a call to action, for whether 'canker' means 'ulcer' or 'maggot' it implies a positive course of remedial action. The question is not one for Horatio to comment directly on, and he reminds Hamlet that the time for effective action is limited:

> *Horatio* It must be shortly known to him from England
> What is the issue of the business there.
> *Hamlet* It will be short: the interim is mine;
> And a man's life's no more than to say 'One'.
>
> (v, 2, 71–4)

'A man's life's no more than to say "One"': in the brevity of life, one can at least achieve a moment of significant, aggressive action. The affirmation of self is the end of life: and *one* denotes, among other things, the unity of self. The word harks back to the meditation on the sentry-platform, and its recognition of the '*one* defect' which may 'Soil our addition; and indeed it takes / From our achievements, though perform'd at height, / The pith and marrow of our attribute.' (I, 4, 20–2) M. M. Mahood's commentary is especially valuable here: '*Addition*, besides being our applied title, is the sum total of our natures, what we add up to in ourselves. *Attribute*, according to the N.E.D., can mean not only a quality ascribed or assigned but an inherent or characteristic quality.'[10] The final implications of these terms, then, are that the 'one' of self must include the 'one defect', together with the sum of our inherent and attributed parts. Clearly, this 'one' cannot be adequately stated with the mere vulgar striking of a blow. Nor can it be expressed through the arts of the stage, though Hamlet had once, in a moment of devastating self-revelation, indicated that these would express him:

> *Hamlet* Would not this, sir, and a forest of feathers – if the rest of my fortunes turn Turk with me – with two Provincial roses on my razed shoes, get me a fellowship in a cry of players, sir?
> *Horatio* Half a share.
> *Hamlet* *A whole one, I.*
>
> (III, 2, 286–91)

Identity can only be an experimental truth. It is confirmed in the moment of equipoise between self and situation, which must include the will to action and the public awareness of the act. The problem, then, is to encounter the moment that offers the opportunity of significant action. And this moment will present itself in the essential form of a challenge.

VI

The challenge takes on the actuality of the King's wager. It is a formal, and symbolic, solution to Hamlet's predicament. Hamlet has previously indicated no plan, but a determination to use the time at his disposal: and his 'I am constant to my purposes, they follow the King's pleasure' is no less than the truth. He will react to the situation that 'special providence' supplies. He must have a dark awareness that in fencing with Laertes he is opposing the 'pass and fell incensed point' of his adversary, the King. The challenge, then, gives Hamlet this: it is an opportunity for the duel, a symbolic yet real combat; it provides an audience, before which he can both vindicate and dramatise himself; and it is the imitation of a great act once performed by his father. The 'union' which is the central pun of the final scene is that of Hamlet himself, as – in death – with Laertes, with Claudius, with his father and mother, the '*one* flesh' to which he had once referred (IV, 3, 54). The sword-play itself proceeds through the phases of symbolic contest, genuine fighting, and the ultimate act of killing the King. We should note that Hamlet does not kill Claudius until Laertes has gasped out the truth. The Court, therefore, knows it too – and apart from cries of 'Treason!' it does nothing to impede Hamlet in his regicide. He acts, then, upon the implied state of public knowledge and sanction – to which his last words enjoin Horatio. In the final minutes of his life,

Hamlet has become King: and tragic hero. 'Il est devenu ce qu'il était.'

And perhaps this, the final position in Hamlet's life, is the answer to the kingly summons of the first scene, 'The bell then beating *one* . . .' Or perhaps we reflect back the soldierly rites of the conclusion into the prime meaning of Hamlet's 'one'. For Hamlet does say it. After the courtesies that precede the duel, Hamlet, willing as ever to react rather than act, invites Laertes to the first attack, 'Come on sir', and Laertes returns the invitation, 'Come my lord'. The rapiers touch then, and we conceive of Hamlet, after that, launching the first attack. The dialogue of the foils, with its staccato interrogations and metallic elisions, is Hamlet's final scanning of his universe. Sooner or later he will pose Laertes a question to which the stock answer will come a fiftieth of a second too late. And then the counter-thrust slides inside its parry, and travels through free space home to its target, *one*.

6 *Troilus and Cressida:* Tempus edax rerum

Troilus and Cressida appears to present itself as a reworking of earlier material in the canon. One is immediately aware of certain correspondences (Troilus/Romeo, Pandarus/Nurse) and of some stylistic reminiscences of Shakespeare's earlier manner. From these resemblances, commentators[1] have been tempted to conclude that the play was conceived, perhaps partly written, at an earlier stage, and rewritten in accordance with a more complex vision. But this surely is erroneous. Shakespeare is drawing on the styles of his former manner to adduce certain characteristics (and inadequacies) of his dramatis personae.[2] In an important sense, *Troilus and Cressida* is a revision of *Romeo and Juliet* (also, of *Henry V*), but not in the sense that most holders of revisionist theories adopt. Rather, it is the act of *seeing again* that every great artist applies to his earlier work in breaking fresh ground. I regard *Troilus and Cressida* as a grand allusion to the earlier treatment of love and war in the canon; and if *Troilus and Cressida* reads like a revaluation, that is no more than a recognition that Time is a presence in the Shakespearean canon, as well as in this play.

I

The subject matter of Troilus and Cressida is love and war: the business of the play is a sustained debate on values, moderated by Time. 'Debate' here takes on a formal and a generalised sense, for the two great Council scenes are emblems of the play's structure, and representative of what the action of the play is constantly doing – proposing, opposing, and redefining values presented for consideration. In no Shakespeare play is the audience so overtly and incessantly asked to *think*, to address itself to the serious questions under discussion. It is agreed that this debate is largely corrosive of the values considered. All stems from the symbolic interdependence of the two major actions: Troy is the archetype of doomed citadels, Troilus the archetype of deceived lovers.[3] Helen and Cressida represent, and subvert, the values associated with love and war. The parallel Q.E.D.s of these propositions are the murder of Hector, and the yielding of Cressida to Diomedes. But the stealthy subversion of values is discernible in the language of even the earliest scenes. The Choric rhetoric is brassy, reverberant, yet 'not in confidence' : Troilus' opening image of love, 'such cruel battle here within', is devastatingly passé, a survival from the Bronze Age of Petrarchanism : Cressida's adept badinage, taken with her soliloquy, is more subtly knowing than the apparently liberated language of the young ladies generally on view in the earlier comedies :[4] the Greek council, for all its formal impressiveness, is in reality a deplorable affair. Agamemnon's rhetoric is as hollow as the Grecian tents : his remedy for failure is that everyone should try harder, a thought that requires thirty lines to utter. Nestor, respectfully emulating his superior in uselessness (the specialty of rule is not neglected here) takes another twenty-seven lines to add that hard times sort out the men from the boys. These two speeches have often been admired[5] – mistakenly, as I think. A major Shakespearean speech cannot be paraphrased. The metaphoric substance defies reduction to prose. But the matter of Agamemnon and Nestor's speeches can readily be presented in banal prose; the tropes are purely ornamental, cosmetic, unconnected with any vital idea. Ulysses, in applauding the speeches of his seniors, is certainly upholding the principle of Order; but the incapacity of the General is plain, and Ulysses tactfully leaves it open for his hearers to take 'The General's disdain'd / By him one step below' (I, 3, 129–30) as instance or actuality. And the Trojans, in at least considering the issues of war and peace, compel us to revise our judgement of the earlier Council scene. The Greeks are fighting for no better an object (the 'honour' of the much derided Menelaus) than the Trojans. Yet they discuss nothing more profound than their disciplinary problems. The strategic direction of this play, then, is marked long before Hector's volte-face in favour of 'our joint and several dignities' (II, 2, 193), and Troilus' easy identification of war with 'fame' (II, 2, 202), a word fully exposed in *Love's Labour's Lost.*[6] The bathetic rhymed couplets terminating the Prologue signal the onset of the acid that eats the substance of this play, until all is consumed.

II

It is the metaphoric area of the play's texture that concerns us here. Much of it need only be touched on. As is well known, *Troilus and Cressida* is distinguished by its image clusters of diseases, animals, and food.[7] The general point made by the imagery of disease and animals is clear enough.[8] They serve to caricature and degrade the activities of the dramatis personae. This use of animal/disease imagery is not peculiar to *Troilus and Cressida*, nor indeed to Shakespeare. Webster, Middleton, Jonson, for instance, are well aware of such metaphoric possibilities. The food images here are given extended prominence, more so to my knowledge than in any contemporary play. Eating and tasting, with their attendant terms, construct a profound metaphor for human activity, and its exploitation in *Troilus and Cressida* goes far to establish an intellectual critique of the actions recorded there.

We can begin with the obvious uses: some of the food-images have no profounder purpose than to sustain an idea stated more importantly elsewhere. People are often equated with food: Pandarus dismisses some anonymous Trojan soldiery as 'chaff and bran, porridge after meat' (I, 2, 262–3). Thersites, to Ajax, is a 'cobloaf' (II, 1, 41) and 'thou vinewedst leaven' (II, 1, 15); to Achilles, 'my cheese, my digestion' (II, 3, 44) and 'thou crusty batch of nature' (V, 1, 6). Troilus, in his defence of honourable election (that is, the need to stand by one's choice) moves strangely from the instance of wife, to silk, to food: 'nor the remainder viands / We do not throw in unrespective sieve, / Because we now are full.' (II, 2, 70–2) The idea that any formally persuasive analogies can be drawn between conduct to wife, and food, dissolves as soon as one considers it. The instance fails as rhetoric, but is worth noting precisely because it is embedded in its metaphoric collective. The same point can be made concerning Troilus'

manhood and honour
Should have hare-hearts, would they but fat their thoughts
With this cramm'd reason . . .
(II, 2, 47–9)

This is image as polemic, good enough for talking down Helenus but for little else. It is, naturally, of a piece with Troilus' immaturity. Generally the food images seem to signal a certain coarseness of spirit, even an intellectual obtuseness, on the part of the dramatis personae. Greeks and Trojans alike incline to the metaphor, as readily as the Venetians in *The Merchant of Venice* to commercial/accounting imagery: it expresses, unmistakably, a collective cast of mind. And the anonymous servant who picks up an ill phrase of Pandarus' voices exactly that sense of queasiness, of distaste, that any audience of sensibility must experience:

Pandarus . . . for my business seethes.
Servant Sodden business! there's a stewed phrase indeed.
(III, 1, 43–4)

From people, to qualities: the food images supply a subtler critique of humanity. Thus Pandarus' question to Cressida: 'Is not birth, beauty, good shape, discourse, manhood, learning, gentleness, virtue, youth, liberality, and such like, the spice and salt that season a man?' (I, 2, 274–9) It is a crude introduction to the materialist reduction of behaviour sketched in during the Helen–Paris–Pandarus conversation:

Paris He eats nothing but doves, love, and that breeds hot blood, and hot blood begets hot thoughts, and hot thoughts beget hot deeds, and hot deeds is love.
Pandarus Is this the generation of love? hot blood, hot thoughts, and hot deeds? Why, they are vipers: is love a generation of vipers?

(III, 1, 140–6)

I emphasise the central importance of this scene. We now have a better understanding of Shakespeare's way of 'presenting', centrally, his major statements,[9] and we can also infer much of his intention from the fact that this is the only scene in which Helen appears. So this scene, perhaps the first in our drama to identify the quality of triviality, is a *reductio ad absurdum* of the war. (And of Troilus' amour in the following scene.) It links also with Priam's view of Paris, 'You have the honey still, but these the gall' (II, 2, 144). Love, the suggestion runs, is no more than a behavioural spasm, the pursuit of its food by the bee.

Ulysses, as we should expect, refines the point. Love requires an object; pride, or self-love, needs only itself; the metaphor remains the same. 'How one man eats into another's pride / While pride is fasting in his wantonness!' (III, 3, 136–7) is his account, to Achilles, of human conduct. Achilles he in fact sees as 'the proud lord / That bastes his arrogance with his own seam' (II, 3, 194–5): for Ajax to go to Achilles would be 'to enlard his fat-already pride' (II, 3, 205). All these are variations on Agamemnon's 'He that is proud eats up himself: pride is his own glass, his own trumpet, his own chronicle; and whatever praises itself but in the deed, devours the deed in the praise' (II, 3, 164–8). Pride is an adverse description of a sense of honour; honour is a national, as well as personal, concept of conduct. Both are subject to interpretation as mere drives, appetites for self-aggrandisement. And the end-product of qualities so undermined is a state of rot and waste: 'like fair fruit in an unwholesome dish, are like to rot untasted.' (II, 3, 128–9) Pride, like desire, is at bottom purely an appetite. So 'appetite' levels a joint accusation at war and love.

The play's central metaphor, when it cannot assault openly, saps and undermines relentlessly. Judgement of people and reputations becomes, with Nestor, 'For here the Troyans taste our dear'st repute / With their fin'st palate' (I, 3, 337–8). Reputation, and with it honour, is established not as an objective fact but as the act of connoisseurship; and 'Now, Ulysses, I begin to relish thy advice' (I, 3, 388) confirms the point. Thus the opinion / value debate (of the Trojan council, especially) is diminished by an image suggestive of wine-tasting : moral values are subsumed in aesthetic. Nor is this view of human conduct confined to Nestor. Diomedes extends it to Paris and Menelaus in his icy résumé of the situation :

> Not palating the taste of her dishonour
> With such a costly loss of wealth and friends :
> He, like a puling cuckold, would drink up
> The lees and dregs of a flat tamed piece :
>
> (IV, 1, 58–61)

Good taste, then, would reject such an object. Diomedes is as central as Thersites to the play; he sees a world in which moral values are effaced, or subservient to a man-of-the-world's aesthetic discrimination. It is the disgust of the dealer for an unworthy art-object, and not a moral repulsion, that Diomedes asserts.

The critique of conduct is not finished yet. The passions, or emotions, are seen as a variety of sensation. Troilus' anticipation of his encounter with Cressida is

> I am giddy; expectation whirls me round.
> The imaginary relish is so sweet
> That it enchants my sense : what will it be,
> When that the watery palate tastes indeed
> Love's thrice repured nectar? death, I fear me,
> Swooning destruction, or some joy too fine,
> Too subtle-potent, tuned too sharp in sweetness,
> For the capacity of my ruder powers :
> I fear it much; and I do fear besides,
> That I shall lose distinction in my joys;
> As doth a battle, when they charge on heaps
> The enemy flying.
>
> (III, 2, 19–30)

The overwhelmingly physical impact of the meeting of Troilus is unsparingly presented here, especially in the conclusion. This conscious epicureanism must modify the general impression that we receive of Troilus, that he is purely an *ingénu*. It is not too difficult to visualise a Troilus translated by time into an aristocratic connoisseur of the flesh.

Cressida affords another aspect of the idea. Her reaction to the news of parting is

> Why tell you me of moderation?
> The grief is fine, full, perfect, that I taste,
> And violenteth in a sense as strong
> As that which causeth it: how can I moderate it?
> If I could temporise with my affection,
> Or brew it to a weak and colder palate,
> The like allayment could I give my grief:
>
> (IV, 4, 2–8)

The physicality of her emotions ('palate' is Troilus' word, too) blends with a sense that she is luxuriating in her grief, making the most of it. It is genuine grief, yet it will pass away; the underlying proposition is 'curae leves loquuntur'. The canker in the rose is identifiable even here, for *temporise* is the linguistic refuge of Time, and Time will soon emerge into the open. Troilus' apprehension is of an 'Injurious Time', who 'scants us with a single famish'd kiss, / Distasted with the salt of broken tears.' (IV, 4, 44–50) This is the reality of the passions: now indeed emotion becomes a sensation, the taste of salt. The metaphor yields to actuality.

The collective force of the metaphors I have traced is a statement that the origins of human behaviour lie in blind appetite. Everywhere the argument is reductionist. Passions become sensations, moral states yield to aesthetic appraisal; humanity in political flux is judged by connoisseurship, and statecraft is the art of the party manager. Love, together with pride and honour, are behavioural spasms. The root of all is appetite: Ulysses detects it as the supreme adversary to Order:

> Then everything includes itself in power,
> Power into will, will into appetite;
> And appetite, an universal wolf,
> So doubly seconded with will and power,
> Must make perforce an universal prey.
> And last eat up himself.
>
> (I, 3, 119–24)

And Hector, too, glimpses the same enemy:

> There is a law in each well-order'd nation
> To curb those raging appetites that are
> Most disobedient and refractory.
> If Helen then be wife to Sparta's king,

> As it is known she is, these moral laws
> Of nature and of nations speak aloud
> To have her back return'd.
>
> (II, 2, 180–6)

The analysis is none the less correct for the improper conclusion that follows. Hector's 'Joint and several dignities' makes national honour (or prestige) itself a kind of appetite. And this consideration erodes all the terms associated with honour. 'The language of Paris' question ("noble", "true", "faith") is the language of the ghost order of value that haunts this world and conflicts so violently with its reality', as Horowitz observes.[10] The metaphor of appetite stamps the ultimate act of the War, Achilles' slaying of a disarmed prisoner : 'My half-supp'd sword, that frankly would have fed, / Pleas'd with this dainty bait, thus goes to bed.' (v, 8, 19–20).

III

The drift of the food and tasting imagery is, then, to subvert human activity and its values. But an entirely different function of the imagery now discloses itself, yet one that tends in the same direction. Essentially, the food images ally themselves with Time. This is the point of the first (and perhaps the most important) of the play's images of food :

> *Pandarus* He that will have a cake out of the wheat must needs tarry the grinding.
> *Troilus* Have I not tarried?
> *Pandarus* Ay, the grinding; but you must tarry the bolting.
> *Troilus* Have I not tarried?
> *Pandarus* Aye, the bolting, but you must tarry the leavening.
> *Troilus* Still have I tarried.
> *Pandarus* Aye, to the leavening; but here's yet in the word 'hereafter' the kneading, the making of the cake, the heating of the oven and the baking; nay, you must stay the cooling too, or you may chance to burn your lips.
>
> (I, 1, 14–26)

The vehicle is food, but the tenor is Time : Time viewed as an inexorable, determined process in which the end is contained in the beginning, the conclusion in the premise. The image thus announced imposes itself upon the drama, for Time, implicit here, becomes an overt presence later.[11] It is perceived by Troilus as his enemy, 'injurious Time' (IV, 4, 44) : to Ulysses, 'Love, friendship, charity, are subjects all / To envious and calumniating Time' (III, 3, 173–4) : to Hector, 'the end crowns all, / And that old common arbitrator, Time, / Will one day end it' (IV, 5, 224–6). These are diverse concepts of Time, and the play does not precisely and cardinally support any one of them. We should certainly expect Renaissance iconography to offer some guidance here, Time being one of the most popular emblematic representations. In fact, Shakespeare, as I judge, steers clear of a precise (and limiting) emblematic identification. There is undoubtedly a ready association between the Time of this play and the Kronos-Saturn tradition of Time the devourer and destroyer. Panofsky notes, of Kronos-Saturn, that 'the mythical tale that he had devoured his own children was said to signify that Time, who had already been termed 'sharp-toothed' by Simonides and *edax rerum* by Ovid, devours whatever he has created.'[12] This is suggestive, and obviously germane to my argument here. But he points to the other major tradition, of Time as revealer and bringer of Truth.[13] Now that seems especially appropriate to the events of v, 2. Moreover, there is a queer subterranean connection between 'Veritas Filia Temporis' and the stage fact that it is Cressida (the 'daughter of the game') who is being revealed to Troilus. These mental linkages supply different perspectives on the action. And I add a third possibility, for Chew has pointed out that 'Justice, like her sister Truth, is often closely associated with Time. Shakespeare calls Time the old "common arbitrator", and again, "the old justice examines all offenders" '.[14] As the first of Chew's instances is drawn from *Troilus and Cressida*, the point is made for me; and 'arbitrator', we can note, appears elsewhere in Shakespeare with the sense of 'that which brings about a definite issue' (*OED*), and associated with justice : 'But now the arbitrator of despairs, / Just death, kind umpire of men's miseries . . .' (*I Henry VI*, II, 5, 28–9). Devourer, revealer, justice : all these aspects of Time are present in Shakespeare's treatment. The play does, however, clearly ally the action of Time with the metaphoric leitmotiv. The association is explicit in Priam's 'As honour, loss of time, travail, expense, / Wounds, friends, and what else dear is consum'd / In hot digestion of this cormorant War' (II, 2, 4–6), and the intensity of the metaphor is stronger even than appears : one remembers Navarre's vain challenge to 'cormorant devouring Time' at the opening of *Love's Labour's Lost*. Cormorant/War/Time is the association, and perhaps Shakespeare sees War as a dramatised expression of Time. Time can be thought of here as an inquisitor, an auditor, the agent of the reality that in Shakespeare ceaselessly questions and challenges the statements of the dramatis personae. Its role is deeply sceptical, rather than essentially destructive.

This is seen in Time's examination of another shadowy presence in *Troilus and Cressida*, the self. It is worth tracing the development of this interrogation. Cressida and Pandarus raise the matter :

Pandarus Do you know a man if you see him?
Cressida Ay, if I ever saw him before and knew him.
Pandarus Well, I say Troilus is Troilus.
Cressida Then you say as I say; for, I am sure, he is not Hector.
Pandarus No, nor Hector is not Troilus in some degrees.
Cressida 'Tis just to each of them; he is himself.
Pandarus Himself! Alas, poor Troilus! I would he were.
Cressida So he is.
Pandarus Condition, I had gone barefoot to India.
Cressida He is not Hector.
Pandarus Himself! no, he's not himself: would 'a were himself!
Well, the gods are above; time must friend or end...
(I, 2, 68–84)

This is mere badinage, a trifling with a common phrase 'to be oneself'; but the collocation with time is significant. The word-play becomes a startlingly penetrative conceit at the Troilus-Cressida encounter:

Troilus What offends you, lady?
Cressida Sir, mine own company.
Troilus You cannot shun yourself.
Cressida Let me go and try:
I have a kind of self resides with you;
But an unkind self, that itself will leave,
To be another's fool.
(III, 2, 152–7)

It is both an anticipation of the general course of the play, and a specific preparation for Ulysses' discourse with Achilles in the following scene. The self is not an absolute and permanent entity, but a dynamic state that changes with different relationships. Cressida-with-Troilus will not be the same as Cressida-with-Diomedes: she knows it, regrets it, but accepts it. Achilles is compelled to take a similar view of his achievements:

Ulysses A strange fellow here
Writes me: 'That man, how dearly ever parted,
How much in having, or without or in,
Cannot make boast to have that which he hath,
Nor feels not what he owes, but by reflection;
As when his virtues shining upon others
Heat them and they retort that heat again
To the first giver.'

Achilles This is not strange, Ulysses.
The beauty that is borne here in the face
The bearer knows not, but commends itself
To others' eyes; nor doth the eye itself,
That most pure spirit of sense, behold itself,
Not going from itself; but eye to eye opposed
Salutes each other with each other's form;
For speculation turns not to itself,
Till it hath travell'd and is mirror'd there
Where it may see itself. This is not strange at all.

Ulysses I do not strain at the position, –
It is familiar, – but at the author's drift;
Who, in his circumstance, expressly proves
That no man is the lord of any thing,
Though in and of him there be much consisting,
Till he communicate his parts to others;
Nor doth he of himself know them for aught
Till he behold them form'd in the applause
Where they're extended; who, like an arch, reverberates
The voice again, or, like a gate of steel
Fronting the sun, receives and renders back
His figure and his heat.

(III, 3, 95–123)

Achilles has already arrived at a cruder and more superficial version of the same idea (III, 3, 74–87), and the dialogue fixes and projects the statement that people exist only through relationships. It is perhaps the main intellectual thesis of *Troilus and Cressida*. The self is an enigma, and there are some odd, throwaway allusions to it. 'The unknown Ajax', for instance, is Ulysses' reference (III, 3, 125). The phrase vibrates strangely, for what could exist in that ox unknown to us? Yet the play rebukes us, for Ajax is the only Greek to express the common, decent impulse of humanity at the news of Hector's death :

If it be so, then bragless let it be;
Great Hector was a man as good as he.
(V, 8, 5–6)

Again, the play is scarcely concerned to plumb the depths of Achilles, yet we are reminded that they exist :

My mind is troubled, like a fountain stirr'd;
And I myself see not the bottom of it.
(III, 3, 311–12)

That is the only hint of the unknown Achilles, yet it is of a piece with the play's account of the disturbingly provisional nature of the human essence.

It seems appropriate, then, that the curiously modern term 'cognition' should appear in *Troilus and Cressida* – its only occurrence in Shakespeare. And it crystallises the intellectual climax of the play:

> *Troilus* Fear me not, sweet lord;
> I will not be myself, nor have cognition
> Of what I feel:
> (v, 2, 62–4)

After this abdication of mind there is no more, essentially, to be said of Troilus.[15] The will interposes between *feeling* and *knowing*: it is his epitaph, and he wrote it, as does everybody in Shakespeare. We need not take the play's verdict to be as drastically pessimist as Troilus assumes, however. Ulysses has lodged a vital objection: 'What hath she done, prince, that can soil our mothers?' (v, 2, 134) Time cannot rewrite its own records, and what is past is secure against Time. And Agamemnon, too, has with a basic decency said something that needed to be said during the truce:

> What's past, and what's to come, is strew'd with husks,
> And formless ruin of oblivion:
> But in this extant moment, faith and troth,
> Strain'd purely from all hollow bias drawing,
> Bids thee with most divine integrity,
> From heart of very heart, great Hector, welcome.
> (iv, 5, 166–71)

The 'extant moment' – the timeless moment, we might call it – carries its own defence against time. Agamemnon means it. He knows that the truce will be followed by more blood, and he knows also that this moment of peace and good fellowship has its own kind of authenticity, one that must be acknowledged. And perhaps we conclude that as the truce is an act of love, so love is a truce in a long war: and so should the moment of faith and troth between Troilus and Cressida have been acknowledged, before the resumption of a war in which Cressida will fall captive, *spoil* to opportunity. The truce is the play's metaphor for the challenge to Time's supremacy, and a maturer Troilus might have understood it.

IV

But Troilus, with his overwhelming subjectivity, is above all the conduit for the experience of the play – experience, that is, defined (in his own terms) as feeling. Troilus' is the voice that laments the defection of Cressida, that responds to Hector's death with defiant hate, that spurns Pandarus. Of course, the play does not identify itself with Troilus. The critique of his conduct is already complete, and Aeneas voices the reaction of embarrassed detachment: 'my lord, you do discomfort all the host' (v, 10, 10). And yet, Troilus' experience is the play's. Troilus' story is one of surfeit and rejection: 'The fragments, scraps, the bits and greasy relics / Of her o'er-eaten faith, are bound to Diomed' (v, 2, 159–60). Appetite itself revolts from its indulgence. Thersites caps this with an image of self-eating: 'What's become of the wenching rogues? I think they have swallowed one another; I would laugh at that miracle: yet, in a sort, lechery eats itself' (v, 4, 34–7). So does Pride (as Agamemnon observed), and so does War: Hector himself, 'Dexterity so obeying appetite, / That what he will, he does' (v, 5, 27–8) has to yield to the stronger appetite of Achilles (stronger, because it can swallow scruples of chivalric conduct that Hector's cannot). 'My half-supp'd sword, that frankly would have fed, / Pleased with this dainty bait, thus goes to bed' (v, 8, 19–20). And the ultimate experience of the self-consuming, self-rejecting appetite is concentrated in the final scene. Aeneas, the voice of cool moderation, has a metaphor that hints at the coming phase in the play's process: 'Never go home: here starve we out the night' (v, 10, 2). The associative idea is that of fasting, after feasting; and Aeneas, who had signalled the end of Troilus' idyll, now heralds the reckoning to come.

The play now winds down rapidly: and it does so with a strange jerkiness not found elsewhere in Shakespeare.[16] One thinks of a falling curtain that sticks as it descends. One thinks, even, of the close to Giraudoux's *La Guerre de Troie n'aura pas lieu*, in which the final curtain begins to descend, then reverses itself as the action takes a final turn. That curtain is a part of Giraudoux's design, and I think we ought to reflect on the ways in which the implied curtain here expresses Shakespeare's plan. 'Hector is dead; there is no more to say' (22) is an invitation to still one's responses. I have seen it played thus, with the curtain there, and it makes *Troilus and Cressida* a heroic tragedy, the figure of Troilus defiant against the darkling walls of the doomed citadel. 'Stay yet . . .' and a final spasm of energy and hate follows. It is purely physical, and it expires in exhaustion. 'Strike a free march to Troy! with comfort go: / Hope of revenge shall hide our inward woe' (30–1). The banality, the total moral bankruptcy of this match the experience of exhaustion. Pandarus enters, an irritant who galvanises a final twitch from the body of Troilus: 'Hence, broker-lackey! ignomy and shame / Pursue thy life, and live aye with thy name' (34–5). And Troilus departs. Surely, now the play can rest, and with it our emotions? But the consequences of the preceding events are not to be spared us. Besides, they are dramatically apposite. We do not *want* Pandarus now. We have grasped the point of the drama, and like Troilus we would rather go. We find Pandarus not funny any longer, but obscene, degrading, tedious. So, when he buttonholes the audience, it completes the experience of revulsion, of being compelled to contemplate the results of surfeit. His talk is of medicine for aching bones, of ease from the pox. Troilus and his lost amour become, in the last perspective, a humble-bee who has lost his honey and sting: 'And being once subdued in armed tail, / Sweet honey and sweet notes together fail' (44–5). Enough, one feels. And the sheer tawdriness of Pandarus' rhymed couplets, both in manner and content, adds the final touch to the experience. 'Even prose has been deflated', as Vickers well observes.[17] My contention, then, is that the prime experience of the final stages is, for the audience, one of surfeit and revulsion. The imagistic narrative points to a physical reckoning after excess; the theatrical response counterpoints that subliminal narrative. The critical discussion of the play's genres – tragicomedy, comedy, intellectual tragedy, and so on – is apt to miss the central point that Shakespeare is making: this play is *sui generis* by denying all genres. It flirts with several, before opting for a final experience that is modelled on the rejection of expectation and desire, and thus on the play's prime metaphor. *Troilus and Cressida* becomes a kind of dramatic bio-destruct. It has consumed its own ideas and emotions relentlessly, and the genres collapse inwards upon themselves.

So *eating* is the main figure for the activities of the dramatis personae: and the figure allies itself with the audience's reception of the play. But the true companion to the metaphor here is Time. It is not often that one has the opportunity to speculate on the imaginative, as opposed to the purely narrative or occasional source of a Shakespeare play; but *Troilus and Cressida* is in this as in other respects an exceptional play. Shakespeare knew his Ovid, both in the original and in Arthur Golding's translation of the *Metamorphoses* in 1567. Geoffrey Bullough, indeed, prints extracts from Books XII and XIII of Golding's translation as a probable source for *Troilus and Cressida*.[18] I point, however, to Book XV, with its long meditation on Time as flux, as the stimulus to Shakespeare's imagination.

Things eb and flow, and every shape is made too passe away.
The tyme itself continually is fleeting like a brooke.

(198–9)

Wee shall not bee the same wee were too day or yisterday.

(237)

And, most conclusively,

Thou tyme, the eater up of things, and age of spyghtfull teene,

Destroy all things.

(258–9)[19]

No doubt the profound associations of Time and consumption are such that they could have occurred independently to two major poetic imaginations. And Time the devourer, as we have seen, was a Renaissance commonplace. Troy, as a classic instance of mutability, contains its own associations. So there is no argument based on probabilities which can assign the imaginative source of *Troilus and Cressida* to Ovid. But it is at least suggestive that the Troy legend and the disquisition on Time are both present in Ovid, if in different books. I cannot pursue the speculation, but am content to read *Troilus and Cressida* as a dramatic meditation on a single epigraph : *tempus edax rerum.*

7 Sexual Imagery in *Coriolanus*

Of sexual interest, in the conventional sense, there is virtually nothing in *Coriolanus*. But an undercurrent of sexual images adds to our 'secret impressions', in Morgann's phrase,[1] of the theme of the play. They provide an insistent suggestion that the concerns of the play are sexual, defined in the broadest sense, or that the mainsprings of the activities depicted are not without sexual implications. The subject-matter of *Coriolanus* is politics and war; but the sexual images imply that a major focus of interest lies elsewhere. The interrelation of war and sex is the underlying statement of the play.

I

We can conveniently begin, as does Shakespeare, with Coriolanus' relations with his mother. The first pronouncement on Coriolanus's motivation is the First Citizen's, 'I say unto you, what he hath done famously, he did it to that end: though soft conscienced men can be content to say it was for his country, he did it to please his mother, and to be partly proud . . .' (I, 1, 38–41). The statement that Coriolanus is dominated by his mother is fully confirmed later; and it indicates that the main actions of Coriolanus' public career, his military victories, have to be regarded as reflexes of the primary human relationship. If we turn to Volumnia, we find that she regards Coriolanus' person and fame as a sort of sexual surrogate: 'If my son were my husband, I should freelier rejoice in that absence wherein he won honours, than in the embracements of his bed, where he would show most love . . .' (I, 3, 4–7). Her pleasure is in her son's victories; but she is implacably opposed to his pleasure being taken anywhere else, and she adds significantly: 'had I a dozen sons, each in my love alike and none less dear than thine and my good Martius, I had rather had eleven die nobly for their country than one voluptuously surfeit out of action' (I, 3, 24–7). 'Voluptuously' identifies a form of independence that Volumnia has no intention of permitting her son.

The idea of war as a quasi-sexual activity is initiated in the battle scenes that follow. Coriolanus urges his troops to re-form and counter-attack with 'If you'll stand fast, we'll beat them to their wives . . .' (I, 4, 41). This is a reminder (made more explicit by Cominius in a later scene; IV, 6, 81–3) of the reward anciently grasped by victorious troops. (It is worth noting that Henry V did not make use of this particular war-cry, but Richard III did.) The matter becomes overt when the victorious Coriolanus greets Cominius:

> Oh! let me clip ye
> In arms as sound as when I woo'd, in heart
> As merry as when our nuptial day was done,
> And tapers burn'd to bedward.
>
> (I, 6, 29–32)

The triumphant battle stirs the recollection of another consummation: the sexual and martial activities are profoundly linked in Coriolanus' mind. And the symbolic values of fighting are, surely, openly revealed when Coriolanus cries delightedly to his troops, 'make you a sword of me?' (I, 6, 76) I suggest that the line can only have a symbolic meaning, that war which Coriolanus came to as an adolescent made him a man, and supplied him with a sense of sexual maturity, the lack of which he is to allude to in the crucial outburst of III, 2, 110–23. It is scarcely fanciful to view Cominius' 'He was a thing of blood' (II, 2, 113) as a description of an initiation rite, a battle-feat which essentially repeats his exploit as a sixteen-year old. But this is to run ahead of the developing insights into Coriolanus' mind that Shakespeare affords. To establish the import of the sexual images for Coriolanus, we have to consider the images of acting. Focused on Coriolanus, a number of references to acting occur in the key scenes of the play. They imply a problem of identity, a man uneasily aware of the possible gap between 'acting' (or seeming) and 'being'. Indeed, the hint of an inner uncertainty is dropped in the opening scene, as Coriolanus says of Aufidius:

> And were I anything but what I am,
> I would wish me only he.
>
> (I, 1, 235–6)

– a wish interestingly paralleled by Aufidius,

> I would I were a Roman; for I cannot,
> Being a Volsce, be that I am.
>
> (I, 10, 4–5)

War provides ready-made models for emulation; usually from one's own side, but often from the enemy (cf., for example, the reputations of Rommel, Marlborough, Lee among their adversaries). It is this that seems to explain Coriolanus's attachment to the reputation of Aufidius – an attachment, nevertheless, expressed via the revealing 'And were I anything but what I am'. And then we find, as has frequently been noted, metaphors of acting used by and of Coriolanus. Cominius' panegyric asserts, 'When he might act the woman in the scene / He proved best man i' th' field . . .' (II, 2, 100–1). Here, as elsewhere in the play, the ambiguity of the verb 'to act' is fully exploited. Coriolanus is at this stage of his career perfectly capable of distinguishing between 'acting' and 'being': 'It is a part / That I shall blush in acting . . .' (II, 2, 148–8). But the inner uncertainty of Coriolanus has in fact been unconsciously acknowledged by Cominius: he 'rewards / His deeds with doing them, and is content / To spend the time, to end it' (II, 2, 131–3). It is true: war provides Coriolanus with a means of identification. It gives him a personal model, and a pursuit; and it is sanctioned by his mother. It simplifies life. Indeed, Coriolanus has no hate for the Volsces – he rather likes them; they are necessary sparring partners. His hate is reserved for the Roman plebeians, who raise problems that cannot be solved in the simplifying war-situation. It is obviously significant that he cannot even remember plebeian names. He can only recollect Brutus and Sicinius of the five tribunes (I, 1, 220–1) and forgets the name of his humble Volscian host altogether. 'By Jupiter! forgot' (I, 9, 90).

II

In the first part of the play, Coriolanus moves successfully through his world. His quarrel with the plebeians is at least temporarily concluded by the coming of war. And war finds Coriolanus in his element. But the people's rejection of Coriolanus brings all the latent problems into the open. His pride, nurtured by his mother, has precipitated the crisis; and now mother withdraws her support.

Coriolanus I muse my mother
Does not approve me further, who was wont
To call them woollen vassals, things created
To buy and sell with groats, to show bare heads
In congregations, to yawn, be still and wonder
When one but of my ordinance stood up
To speak of peace or war.
(III, 2, 7–13)

Mother, of course, has got the point: the point is power, and pride comes after it, not before. And so, in response to Coriolanus's anguished

Would you have me
False to my nature? Rather say I play
The man I am.

(III, 2, 14–16)

Volumnia answers

Oh sir, sir, sir,
I would have had you put your power well on
Before you had worn it out . . .

(III, 2, 16–18)

and then, the stab that only she can deliver :

You might have been enough the man you are,
With striving less to be so . . .

(III, 2, 19–20)

It is a part of the deadly insult that Aufidius finds at the last, 'boy'; we receive an ineffaceable impression of strenuous immaturity, of a youngster trying too hard to prove his manhood.

If Coriolanus suggests an underlying uncertainty – as how could he otherwise, given his mother – Volumnia is perfectly defined. For her, sex is a factor of power; and the sexual note underlies her elegant explanation of the shifts a power-figure must submit to. Coriolanus must speak

But with such words that are but roted in
Your tongue, though but bastards and syllables
Of no allowance . . .

(III, 2, 55–7)

The idea of words as unacknowledged bastards reinforces our impression of the frame of Volumnia's mind. She reaches majestically for a formula that apparently includes, but in fact excludes, the other sexually-related figures in his life :

I would dissemble with my nature where
My fortunes and my friends at stake requir'd
I should do so in honour : I am in this
Your wife, your son . . .

(III, 2, 62–5)

She will speak for Coriolanus's partner and posterity. Power, with her, is the dominant of personal and sexual relations; and the word is on her lips with her clinching injunction to her son, 'As thou hast power and person' (III, 2, 86).

For her son, the maternal order constitutes a breach with what he had conceived to be his nature. Had he been the man of certainty and solidity he appears to the world, he could well have accepted Volumnia's advice: 'perform a part / Thou hast not done before' (III, 2, 109–10). No discredit attaches to actors who act, for good reasons, what they are not. But Coriolanus's reply makes plain the grounds of his deep repulsion from this part:

> Well, I must do't:
> Away my disposition, and possess me
> Some harlot's spirit! My throat of war be turn'd,
> Which quired with my drum, into a pipe
> Small as an eunuch, or the virgin voice
> That babies lulls asleep! The smiles of knaves
> Tent in my cheeks, and school-boys' tears take up
> The glasses of my sight . . .
> I will not do't
> Lest I surcease to honor mine own truth,
> And by my body's action teach my mind
> A most inherent baseness.
>
> (III, 2, 110–17, 120–3)

Why should Coriolanus fear that his body's action will corrupt his mind? The answer, surely, lies in the preceding imagery: the images of impotence, virginity and weeping schoolboys. The wounds of adolescence have never, for Coriolanus, healed.

Wyndham Lewis is, I believe, right in asserting that 'the child-parent situation is the mechanism of the piece . . .'[2] The triangular pattern of dominant mother, dominated son, and the quiet and (at least apparently) submissive wife is a convincing one. Even without Plutarch's statement that Martius 'at her (Volumnia's) desire took a wife also, by whom he had two young children, and yet never left his mother's house therefore',[3] we would note that Vergilia is just the wife that Volumnia would approve of; not an obvious competitor. (That Vergilia represents a set of values powerfully attractive to Coriolanus is very delicately and plausibly argued by Una Ellis-Fermor.)[4] It emerges, from Act III, Scene 2 especially, that Coriolanus' character is partly undeveloped, and that its manifestations are very considerably the product of early drilling: the impossible pride, the contempt for social inferiors, the lack of contact with the realities of social interaction. But the grown man cannot respond to the order, 'about turn'; and Volumnia, in asserting both the fact of dominance and the issuing of orders felt to be unnatural, jars open the unhealed wounds. It follows from this that we can hardly see his character as 'monolithic'[5] or compare him with the 'oak'.[6] I prefer to take the soldier's appraisal as of Aufidius against Coriolanus: 'The worthy fellow is our General: he's the rock, the oak not to be wind-shaken' (v, 2, 116–17). The accented word is 'our', and the judgement is sound. Whatever Aufidius's capacities as a military athlete, he has the character to dispose of his rival.

III

And so Coriolanus is driven into a situation where he cannot act the part of popular leader successfully, because nothing in his upbringing has prepared him for it. Yet his mother compels him to humble himself before the Roman mob. It is the first of the two great hammer blows, both delivered by his mother, that destroy him. His first reaction to the disaster of banishment is deceptively controlled, the words perhaps revealing a shakiness that the voice does not: 'I shall be loved when I am lack'd' (IV, 1, 15). *Love* from the Roman crowd? The Coriolanus of the first three Acts would never have used the word in that context. There is a suggestion here that he needed the support and affection of Rome far more than he had dreamed. The matter is given another curiously sexual twist, when a commentator, Nicanor, observes: 'I have heard it said, the fittest time to corrupt a man's wife, is when she's fallen out with her husband' (IV, 3, 32–4). This is yet another of the recurring hints that we are to evaluate the events in Coriolanus's career in a mode that is not politics, and not the simple psychology of pride and incapacity to feign. The alternative relationship then looms: a conjunction with Aufidius, together with a revenge upon Rome. The Aufidius relationship is subtly delineated. Perhaps the main element has already been indicated by Coriolanus, in his Act I encounter with Aufidius: 'Let the first budger die the other's slave . . .' (I, 8, 7). Dominance is what both seek. And, in conformity to a well-known principle of animal and human psychology, submission gains an instant access of good-will. Both Coriolanus and Aufidius welcome the alliance. Coriolanus, as his soliloquy makes clear, rationalises the matter as a chance of politics:

> Oh world, thy slippery turns! Friends now fast sworn,
> Whose double bosoms seem to wear one heart,
> Whose hours, whose bed, whose meal and exercise
> Are still together: who twin as 'twere in love,
> Unseparable, shall within this hour,

On a dissension of a doit, break out
To bitterest enmity: so, fellest foes,
Whose passions, and whose plots have broke their sleep
To take the one the other, by some chance,
Some trick not worth an egg, shall grow dear friends
And interjoin their issues.

(IV, 4, 12–22)

The point here is not so much the intense evocation of friendship, and the conclusion that foes too could be in that position; it is the shrugging-off of responsibility, the inner myopia, the attribution of the situation to bad luck, 'some trick not worth an egg'. It serves, at all events, to compose Coriolanus's mind for the submission. Aufidius, predictably, is delighted:

Oh Marcius, Marcius;
Each word that thou has spoke, hath weeded from my heart
A root of ancient envy...
Let me twine
My arms about that body...
Know thou first,
I lov'd the maid I married; never man
Sigh'd truer breath. But that I see thee here
Thou noble thing, more dances my rapt heart,
Than when I first my wedded mistress saw
Bestride my threshold.

(IV, 5, 107–9, 112–13, 119–24)

The greeting mirrors that of his aristocratic alter ego (cf. Coriolanus' welcome of Cominius in I, 6, 29–32). In the light of the other images, this message cannot be dismissed as mere hyperbole – a mode, in any case, foreign to this play. Both Aufidius and Coriolanus react to victory with a metaphor of heterosexual triumph. We can certainly regard this as a further manifestation of the sex-war link in this play. But there is another possibility that requires mention at this point. It is here that Shakespeare suggests, though he does not state, the possibility of a homosexual attachment between Aufidius and Coriolanus. It is left undefined, hovering between the possibilities of an attraction specific to these two, and of a general outcome of personalities reared in the aristocratic code and devoted to the activity of war. The matter is heavily underscored in the following scene – we should always pay particular attention to gossip from the servants' quarter when Shakespeare provides it: *Third Servant*. 'Our General himself makes a mistress of him; sanctifies himself with's hand, and turns up the white o' th' eye to his discourse' (IV, 5, 202–4). This is a broad enough hint. And Shakespeare moves a little later to a general appraisal of the nature of war and peace, putting the most acute observations of the play into the mouths of these same servants' hall-philosophers.

First Servant Let me have war, say I; it exceeds peace as far as day does night: it's sprightly, waking, audible, and full of vent. Peace is a very apoplexy, lethargy; mulled, deaf, sleepy, insensible; a getter of more bastard children than war's a destroyer of men.

Second Servant 'Tis so: and as war, in some sort, may be said to be a ravisher, so it cannot be denied, but peace is a great maker of cuckolds.

First Servant Ay, and it makes men hate one another.

Third Servant Reason, because they then less need one another. The wars for my money.

(IV, 5, 237–48)

We need no other text to serve for an explication of *Coriolanus.* There it is: sex is seen as an alternative to war; war is seen as a sexual displacement-activity, a communal therapy and a communal bond. It is, on the whole, rather more depressing than anything in *King Lear.* And there is nothing in the following scenes to contradict it: Cominius, indeed, spells out the immediate application of these propositions to the dumbfounded radicals:

> You have holp to ravish your own daughters, and
> To melt the city leads upon your pates,
> To see your wives dishonour'd to your noses.
>
> (IV, 6, 81–3)

It closes up the hint thrown out by Coriolanus in I, 4, 41. In the aftermath of victory, war yields rapidly to sex.

IV

But the final Act is reserved primarily for the private tragedy of Coriolanus. Names, significantly, become now more important than ever:

Menenius Coriolanus
He would not answer to; forbad all names;
He was a kind of nothing, titleless,

> Till he had forg'd himself a name o' th' fire
> Of burning Rome.
>
> (v, 1, 11–15)

He is, as Maurice Charney remarks, 'peculiarly oppressed by the reality of words';[7] 'Coriolanus' is a profoundly significant title, to be renounced now that he will find a new identity and title in the destruction of Rome. But to destroy Rome he must destroy his mother too. This he tries to affirm:

> Wife, mother, child, I know not, my affairs
> Are servanted to others . . .
>
> (v, 2, 28–9)

But the great confrontation-scene breaks him down.

> I melt, and am not
> Of stronger earth than others. My mother bows,
> As if Olympus to a molehill should
> In supplication nod: and my young boy
> Hath an aspect of intercession, which
> Great nature cries, 'Deny not'. Let the Volsces
> Plough Rome, and harrow Italy: I'll never
> Be such a gosling to obey instinct, but stand
> As if a man were author of himself,
> And knew no other kin.
>
> (v, 3, 28–36)

The gap between instinct and role opens wide; Coriolanus is reduced to the admission – significantly different from the earlier ones – not that he cannot play the part, but that he does not know it:

> Like a dull actor now, I have forgot my part,
> And I am out, even to a full disgrace.
>
> (v, 3, 40–2)

Volumnia takes over. Her annihilating rhetoric crushes Coriolanus' will to pursue the path he had chosen. Her success has been described as 'the victory of love';[8] it seems to me, rather, a simple capitulation, the victory of the stronger over the weaker. For Coriolanus it is defeat absolute; his only chance – of finding identity, never happiness – lay in the decisive pursuit of his course, the attainment of his role. And his final words to his mother speak not of love, but of fear:

Oh my mother, mother! O!
You have won a happy victory to Rome;
But for your son, believe it, oh, believe it,
Most dangerously you have with him prevail'd,
If not most mortal to him.

(v, 3, 185–9)

Coriolanus cannot defeat Volumnia, 'tread . . . on thy mother's womb' (v, 3, 123–4). It is in this that lies the irony of Volumnia's own 'This fellow had a Volscian to his mother' (v, 3, 178) – a line of infinite reverberations. And the identification of Rome with Volumnia is made complete in the aftermath: she is indeed 'our patroness, the life of Rome' (v, 5, 1).

v

Act v, Scene 3 contains the climax to the destruction of Coriolanus, but the play is wound up as a matter arising from his relationship with Aufidius. It has already been made clear that Aufidius has fallen out of love with Coriolanus, as soon as he discovered that he was not the dominant partner in the relationship:

Aufidius He bears himself more proudlier,
Even to my person, than I thought he would
When first I did embrace him.

(iv, 7, 8–10)

This is the only direct motive given for Aufidius's policy, and it reinforces the idea – strongly represented in the words of Volumnia and Coriolanus – that the basic human motivation is the urge to dominate.

If, however, we wish to pursue the suggestion of a homosexual attachment between Aufidius and Coriolanus, we find nothing so overtly stated as the power-theme. There are hints, but these are of more use to the director of the play than the analyst. It is certainly possible to extend the homosexual interpretation through such hints as Aufidius gives, when he ambiguously refers in the final scene to Coriolanus' 'Seducing so my friends' (v, 6, 24) and asserts that he 'Gave him way / In all his own desires' (v, 6, 32–3). This species of sexual suggestion without open statement is not uncommon in Shakespeare: cf., for instance, the dialogue between Macbeth and Lady Macbeth (i, 7, 35–80). It is even possible to read an additional latent insult in Aufidius' final 'boy': that is, the word bears the implication not only of 'servant', but of 'pathic', the passive sexual partner of the dominant Aufidius. Support for this conjecture is available from *Troilus and Cressida*, where Thersites has this observation to make of Patroclus' function:

> *Thersites* Prithee, be silent, boy; I profit not by thy talk: thou art thought to be Achilles' male varlet.
> *Patroclus* Male varlet, you rogue! What's that?
> *Thersites* Why, his masculine whore.
>
> (*Troilus and Cressida*, v, 1, 15–18)

Thersites' collocation of 'boy' and 'male varlet' is interesting as a possible gloss on Coriolanus' infuriated reaction to 'boy':

> and his own notion –
> Who wears my stripes impress'd upon him; that
> Must bear my beating to his grave – shall join
> To thrust the lie unto him.
>
> (v, 6, 107–10)

If we read 'into', the reply to the covert charge is even clearer: Coriolanus asserts that he, not Aufidius, was the dominant partner in the relationship. The lines can be interpreted in two ways by those who accept the homosexual drift: Coriolanus is rebutting a general slander on his sexual proclivities; or he is asserting that notwithstanding Aufidius' claims, he used Aufidius as his pathic.

However, I believe all this to be a trail artfully laid by Shakespeare as a man of the theatre, and one concerned with leaving the actors as much licence in performance as possible.[9] He is suggesting the ambiguities of a relationship, not making a definitive statement. There is no need to go beyond the main essence of the Aufidius–Coriolanus relationship as it is specifically presented, a power-struggle based on personal rivalry. (The relationship, it is worth adding, is curiously similar to Hotspur–Douglas in *Henry IV, Part I*. The same pattern emerges there, of the male aristocrats' mutual-admiration alliance, based on the submission of Douglas, and extended into the rather obvious irrelevance of Lady Percy in Hotspur's life. Clearly, Shakespeare's interest in the characteristics of the Hotspur-type did not cease at Shrewsbury. Achilles continues it; and Coriolanus is an extended investigation into the species.) The final scene of *Coriolanus* reads perfectly well as a cold-blooded destruction by Aufidius of his rival's pretensions, a course indicated as early as I, 10, 15–16. Aufidius, knowing his man, seeks first to deprive Coriolanus of his name, and thus of his identity:

> Ay Marcius, Caius Marcius: dost thou think
> I'll grace thee with that robbery, thy stol'n name
> Coriolanus in Corioles?
> (v, 6, 88–90)

He then supplies his own interpretation of the actions of Coriolanus:

> *Aufidius* but at his nurse's tears
> He whin'd and roar'd away your victory,
> That pages blush'd at him, and men of heart
> Look'd wondering each at others.
> *Coriolanus* Hear'st thou, Mars?
> *Aufidius* Name not the god, thou boy of tears!
> (v, 6, 97–101)

The title not only of Coriolanus, but of Mars, once given him by Aufidius (IV, 5, 124) is now stripped from him, and he is rated as a mother's boy, a Venus-dominated Cupid unfit to stand in the ranks of men. It is, in the deepest sense, a sexual insult, since it cuts at his manhood. 'Coriolanus' was not only a name, but an identity; and the alternative, which was 'Romanus', had been forbidden by his mother. The point about Aufidius's charge is that it is perfectly true. And Coriolanus' last maddened words are an affirmation of what he did, undirected by his mother, 'alone'.

The sexual images, references, and hints in the play seem to have several functions. First, they provide a plain (and to my mind unequivocal) statement that war is a quasi-sexual activity, or that sex and aggression are profoundly linked. I regard the servants' dialogue in IV, 5 as a virtually 'unfiltered' statement of a theme that the imagery has repeatedly suggested. Next, they throw light on the characters of several of the dramatis personae, and especially supply an important part of the puzzle of Coriolanus's mind. The imagery suggests that for him too war is a manifestation of sex, and that both together must be considered as related to his problem of identity. Thus the sexual imagery is linked with the repeated actor's images, all of them centred on Coriolanus – or, by contrast, on Volumnia. Finally, the sexual images, in revealing the bent of Volumnia's disposition, suggest through her a further general statement on sex. For Volumnia sex is part of the mechanism of power; her boy exists to fulfil her needs. She is the one triumphant figure that survives the play, the saviour of Rome. There is an astringent irony in the juxtaposition of the two final scenes – the fêted mother, the butchered son. The honours that she had once preferred even to the 'embracements of his bed' are hers. 'Welcome, ladies, welcome' (v, 5, 6).

The ironic effect of this tiny scene would be infinitely greater if it were staged after the death of her son; but are Shakespeare's intentions any less clear for making her triumph the penultimate scene?

In all major Shakespearean drama, I suggest, he intends us to look where possible for causation: to look beyond Othello to Iago, beyond Iago to Iago's corrupter. Applied to *Coriolanus*, this means that we must look beyond the public issues to the private, and among the private issues look to Volumnia for the origins of the play's action. The main public issue is a mindless war; in no other play does Shakespeare spend such little time on the formal motivations of the war. In the histories he spends much time, if sceptically, on the claims that can be advanced for the justice of this or that war. But in *Coriolanus*, the Romans fight because they are attacked ('the Volsces are in arms', I, 1, 228) and the Volsces fight because they fight (I, 2); not even a token justification is written in. The play becomes then an extended analysis of Coriolanus's reaction to the news – 'I am glad on 't' (I, 1, 229); and to establish this analysis, we must turn to the dominant formative influence in his life. From Volumnia, we derive a strong impression of the interlinked impulses of sex and power. Her son, 'my good Marcius', resorts to war as a means of compensating for sexual uncertainty. Both he and Aufidius find the key issue of war to be an imposition of their will upon their major rival. In all this, the images of heterosexual activity hold in general metaphoric status. (The main exceptions are the servants' dialogue, and Cominius' blunt account of the aftermath of defeat.) They pose, therefore, a familiar question: is the metaphor a means of illuminating the central activity of the play, war and politics, or is the metaphor the true focus of Shakespeare's game? The question is unanswerable: and we can no more resolve the sex-power-drive distinction today than could Shakespeare. It seems best to put it that Shakespeare's quarry is neither tenor nor vehicle, but *the situation*, which comprises tenor and vehicle. Beyond that, we can fall back upon the position that the play's main emphasis is upon the foreground, the unending struggle of human beings to dominate one another. And in this play Shakespeare's verdict on the mainsprings of human action is not, perhaps, very different from the one that Thomas Hobbes was to voice some forty years later: 'So that in the first place, I put for a general inclination of all mankind, a perpetual and restless desire of power after power, that ceaseth only in death.'[10]

8 *The Tempest*

Given that metaphor is the pursuit of meaning via association, *The Tempest* is the supreme Shakespearean model of metaphor in action. The play demonstrates this not through the accumulation of figures classifiable as metaphor (*Troilus and Cressida* is the major instance) but rather through its dramatic essence, which is the experience of half-perceiving, half-grasping for truth. It is natural that this quality of *The Tempest* should lead to so much allegorical criticism. Dowden observed a long time ago that the play 'has had the quality, as a work of art, of setting its critics to work as though it were an allegory; and forthwith it baffles them, and seems to mock them for supposing that they had power to pluck out the heart of its mystery.'[1] That is an observation of fact. But today's critics have largely renounced the task of describing a finite system of correspondences, which is what 'allegory' indicates. Nuttall's position, 'The mystery is never allowed to harden into an ontological dogma',[2] is in harmony with current thinking. I agree with this, and would merely stress that the *possibility* of allegory is part of the intellectual experience of the play that we still acknowledge. It could scarcely be otherwise, when we contemplate an action centred on a being in command of everything save the mental responses of his subjects, and we receive insistent impressions of varying correspondences – Prospero as God, as impresario, as schoolmaster, for instance. Each of these possibilities implies a structure of correspondences radiating out from it. Our intellectual impression, then, is that if at a given point we could stop the action and concentrate on the uppermost association in our minds, we could manufacture a coherent schema round it. But the play moves on and the kaleidoscope shifts.

Now this intellectual impression is fully confirmed by the sensory experience of the play. It is a sustained series of demi-perceptions and mixed reactions. The island itself is full of half-heard sounds, as Caroline Spurgeon noted.[3] What we hear as Ariel's song (II, 1, 300–5) is for Antonio and Sebastian the bellowing of animals, for Alonso 'nothing', for Gonzalo 'a humming, / And that a strange one too.' Then, vision: the island appears enchanting to Gonzalo, 'How lush and lusty the grass looks! how green!' (II, 1, 52) To Antonio and Sebastian it is 'tawny. / With an eye of green in 't' (II, 1, 53–4). Similarly with the air, which to Adrian 'breathes upon us here most sweet', and to the conspirators 'As if it had lungs and rotten ones. / Or as 'twere perfumed by a fen' (II, 1, 46–8). It's a dialogue of perceptions; and the perceptual machine of this play records diverse reactions and mixed judgments. And this sensory puzzlement extends to the synaesthetic images of the later stages: 'As they smelt music' (IV, 1, 178); 'I drink the air before me' (V, 1, 102); 'You do yet taste / Some subtilties o' th' isle' (V, 1, 123–4), 'subtilties' being a decorative, sugared confection. Yet underlying these sensory confusions is an attempt to make sense of the experiences, to clarify the perceptions; and on this level, the play is a movement from Prospero's 'The fringed curtains of thine eye advance / And say what thou seest yond' (I, 2, 406–7), (with its suggestion of the eye peering *through* a curtain) to his

> Their understanding
> Begins to swell, and the approaching tide
> Will shortly fill the reasonable shore
> That now lies foul and muddy.
> (V, 1, 79–82)

Broadly, then, the play moves through conflicting sensations and demi-perceptions towards the *experience* of understanding; though what it is that has been understood might puzzle us, as much as the Boatswain, to relate.

I

That is one way of getting at *The Tempest*. The task of describing what we feel we understand remains. Of what, in terms of meaning rather than impression – if we can hazard this distinction – does the substance of *The Tempest* consist? The best-organised assault upon the play's inner citadel is still, I believe, Reuben Brower's categories. 'The six main continuities, roughly labelled to indicate their character, are: "strange-wondrous", "sleep-and-dream", "sea-tempest", "music-and-noise", "earth-air", "slavery-freedom", and "sovereignty-conspiracy." '[4] The element common to all these continuities is change: 'We can now realise that metamorphosis is truly the key metaphor to the *drama*, and not the key metaphor to a detachable series of decorative analogies.'[5] 'Thus *The Tempest* is, like Marvell's 'Garden', a Metaphysical poem of metamorphosis, though the meaning of change is quite different for the two writers.'[6] These continuities are not in themselves challengeable. The categories are there, in the text. Nor do I challenge the description of the play as a metaphysical poem of metamorphosis. But we can surely go further. And that means, in this context, reaching for a priority among the continuities. We can give ourselves to the whirling, vertiginous oppositions of *The Tempest* and say, this is the play, all is impression and conflict and crossed-category sensation : the total play is a blurred intimation of truth. Or we can search for some basis of meaning, some ground on which to stand. To assert, with what reasons one can adduce, the primacy of a given category here is at least to ensure a view, a perspective of the eye of *The Tempest.* No doubt one can stand elsewhere, and see much, of this metaphysical open-stage drama. But I prefer to identify my standpoint, and report what is visible to me from it.

Much the most important of Brower's categories appears to me the double opposition, slavery–freedom and sovereignty–conspiracy. We can conveniently unite these oppositions in 'power', or 'politics', and take it on from there. It is a standing curiosity of *Tempest* criticism that commentators have been so consistently averse from discussing the political aspect of the play. The overwhelming weight of critical investigation in modern times has been conducted through myth and symbol, allegory, pastoral, romance. Hardly anybody who publishes a volume on Shakespeare's histories thinks to add an epilogue or appendix on *The Tempest.* A recent work entitled *Shakespeare's Political Plays* ignores *The Tempest.* Yet the exercise of power is the manifest content of the bulk of the action. It comes almost as a shock to encounter Witold Ostrowski's epitome of *The Tempest,* 'a story of a struggle for power among men with different political attitudes';[7] and Professor Ostrowski is fully justified in the title of his paper, 'A forgotten meaning of *The Tempest*'. Let us glance at the immediate grounds for this view.

The prime justification for seizing on the political aspect is one of plot, and quantity. The main action concerns Prospero's manipulation of his subjects, together with his defeat of an attempted conspiracy. The Ferdinand–Miranda relationship – which in part is covered by the preceding generalisation – occupies some twenty per cent only of the action. Then, I point to the extraordinary degree to which the dialogue – in the opening scenes especially, giving a 'fix' on the play – is impregnated with terms that denote subordination and mastery in the most unequivocal way. Extended quotation is unnecessary, and I cite only the leading counters. In the first scene we have Master : boatswain : king : counsellor : command : authority. In the second, god : Duke of Milan : King of Naples : a prince of power : government : royalty : lorded : tribute : homage : coronet : crown : subject : minister : schoolmaster : tutor : parent. The Stephano-Trinculo-Caliban encounter adds lieutenant : standard : tyrant : lord : king : queen :

viceroy : grace. The range is enormous, and extends from such tactical variations as 'dry for sway' and 'master of this design' to the occasional immediate metaphor, 'Thou dost here usurp / The name thou ow'st not' (I, 2, 453–4) and 'I will supplant some of your teeth' (III, 2, 57). The source of the action is throughout presented as Prospero's 'art'. Heavily emphasised, 'art' means 'the disciplined exercise of virtuous knowledge'[8] It is associated with 'power', which the others experience as the crude effect of Prospero's 'art' : Caliban supplies the distinction, 'His art is of such power' (I, 2, 372). The central force of all this is inescapable. Our minds are bombarded with a variety of terms which stimulate, indeed compel us to receive the action in terms of power and subordination.

II

The language of *The Tempest* asserts 'power', in the broadest sense, to be the subject of the dramatic discourse. But within this area certain categories are discernible. I perceive three main groups. The first is purely social, the hierarchies that man has evolved for his own government : duke, counsellor, servant. The second is familial. It is introduced analogously by Prospero himself, 'Like a good parent' (I, 2, 94), but elsewhere the play is directly concerned with father–child relationships. The final group is divine power. Prospero refers to 'Providence divine' (I, 2, 159), and it is the unseen presence which the play, both by analogy and by occasional reference, acknowledges. The word 'power' is sometimes linked with divinity. 'Had I been any god of power' says Miranda (I, 2, 10); and more interestingly, Ariel (spokesman here for Prospero) says

for which foul deed
The powers, delaying, not forgetting, have
Incens'd the seas and shores, yea all the creatures
Against your peace.
(III, 3, 72–5)

Prospero's power ('art') has mutated into 'the powers', i.e. divine retribution. Through his agent, Prospero seems to be claiming an identity between divine retribution and his power. Gonzalo's 'Some heavenly power / Guide us' (V, 1, 105–6) extends the suggestion. But I do not wish to press hard upon a single passage. I suggest that we are led to become aware of three levels at which power is exercised – familial, social, and supra-human; and it follows that we may be led to see these levels existing as analogies to the others. This, in addition to the explicit ligatures that Shakespeare has provided ('Like a good parent', 'the powers'). But we are not compelled to expound a system of analogous meanings. Allegory obliges us to identify conclusions: I go no farther than posit an awareness of central analogical possibilities which the play creates in us. Moreoever, the broad import of the action is surely other than theological. The 'Providence' references remind the audience that man is a being exercising his power under God; they assert the religious dimension to human experience. But the action is overwhelmingly concerned with the human, or terrestrial implications of power.[9]

How – aside from Prospero's manipulations – does 'power' cover the Ferdinand–Miranda relationship? Shakespeare demonstrates the connection with a single metaphoric ligature: 'They are both in either's pow'rs' (I, 2, 450). This is characteristic of the mature Shakespearean technique with metaphors. He employs a term not in an overtly or aggressively figurative manner. Rather, he enlarges the sense of the original word by employing it in a new context, so that a word perceived to be literal takes on fresh meanings and possibilities. He thus illuminates the new context, the energy in 'power' being transmitted to the new field. The vital word, unspoken in Prospero's line here, is 'love'; and the conceptual proposition is that love is a kind of power.

Ferdinand and Miranda explore some of the implications. Ferdinand early recognises the paradox that love creates a desired prison for him:

all corners else o' th' earth
Let liberty make use of; space enough
Have I in such a prison.
(I, 2, 491–3)

In their scene together, Ferdinand speaks of the 'bondage' of love (III, 1, 41), and then, together, they parse love in the categories of social subordination and equality:

Miranda I am your wife, if you will marry me;
If not, I'll be your maid: to be your fellow
You may deny me; but I'll be your servant,
Whether you will or no.
Ferdinand My mistress, dearest;
And I thus humble ever.
Miranda My husband, then?
Ferdinand Ay, with a heart as willing
As bondage e'er of freedom: here's my hand.
(III, 1, 83–9)

So Ferdinand and Miranda, surrendering to each other, assert the absolute power of love; and Ferdinand would gain a father to execute all matters of temporal command: 'Let me live here ever; / So rare a wond'red father and a wise / Makes this place Paradise' (IV, 1, 122–4). It is a dream of Paradise, or more precisely a statement that Paradise contains a father. But in this play reality breaks through dreams – it is *The Tempest's* dialectic – and before the close, Ferdinand and Miranda are discovered playing at chess. That symbol of abstract conflict is in effect a training-match, a preparation for the time of political realities when they have to direct the struggle, alone. 'Ludimus effigiem belli', said Vida in his *Scacchia Ludus*, supplying a sense of the icon that commentators of *The Tempest* are customarily reluctant to expound.[10] However harmonious in its immediate context, the game is a covert reminder of the post-*Tempest* world that must follow the death of the benign ruler and father.[11]

III

Love, then, is here a mutation of power. But let us return to the main line of the analysis. There is clearly no difficulty in accounting in general terms for the Stephano–Trinculo–Caliban action. It mimicks the major concerns and events of the play, most obviously the Antonio-Sebastian conspiracy. In the rapid movement from Caliban's 'I prithee, be my god' to 'I'll swear myself thy subject' and 'Thou shalt be lord of it' the frame of reference shifts from burlesque theology to burlesque politics. More than that, the placing of this comic opera revolution is suggestive. It occupies the central scene (III, 2) always a position worth investigation in Shakespeare.[12] The formal act of presentation advances the buffoons. And the very centre of the scene, so far as I can determine, is Stephano's striking of Trinculo. Let us say, then, that the central event in *The Tempest* is a grotesquely misapplied exercise of authority; surely an additional indication of what the play is 'about'. And it directs us, naturally, to reflect on what constitutes true authority. In sum, the Stephano–Trinculo–Caliban episodes compose an anti-masque of power.

That is a judgement on the collective force of those scenes. Individually, the mutineers pose different problems. In the play's miniature sociology, Stephano and Trinculo are simply unregenerate man, the sweepings of Naples. Their unchanging prose is the line of their moral development. They are essentially a social problem: 'Two of these fellows you / Must know and own' says Prospero (V, 1, 274–5). They are to be administered, rather than governed. In the play's texture, they constitute a coarse human fibre out of which it will be remarkably difficult to construct a Utopia. Caliban, as everyone recognises, is different.

Caliban, in bald terms, is the greatest single problem of Prospero's government. This is true on all levels, from the superficial to the most profound; he is Prospero's great challenge and antagonist. Perhaps the best route to understanding his place in the play's design is through reflection on a certain sequence of words: power, potent, potential. The first two words are present in the text of *The Tempest*; the third is not. Its essence suffuses the play. *Potential* I suggest as a way of conceptualising what Shakespeare is addressing himself to here.

'Potential' is the power of man, the power to realise himself fully as a moral, social and artistic being. It will generally be agreed that Prospero is the most advanced study in the canon of such a being. And he himself regards Caliban as the supreme human difficulty to be encountered. The others he can adjure, manipulate, out-manœuvre, simply order. None, not even Antonio, creates in him such bitterness as Caliban.

> A devil, a born devil, on whose nature
> Nurture can never stick; on whom my pains,
> Humanely taken, all, all lost, quite lost;
> (IV, 1, 188–90)

> . . . this demi-devil –
> For he's a bastard one – had plotted with them
> To take my life . . . this thing of darkness I
> Acknowledge mine.
> (V, 1, 272–6)

It is the most humiliating, the most rankling of failures: the rejection of the teacher by his pupil, the governor by his subject, even the father by his incorrigible son. Why does it matter so much? Because Caliban is himself someone of great reality, someone who matters; and because, at bottom, his rejection of Prospero constitutes a criticism of Prospero. He is, if you like, 'Shakespeare's intuition of the untamed beast in man.'[13] But he is much else too. Here I think it essential to avoid dismissing Caliban as a savage, or sentimentalising him as a victim of colonial oppression.[14] Caliban has a case, and he states it; so has Prospero; the matter is maintained in balance. What is plain is Caliban's growth throughout the play. From a mere recalcitrant savage in his opening scene, he grasps his first chance to follow a leader who will conduct him to liberty; and already, under the stimulus of hope, he shows a naturalist's knowledge and love of the island ('I'll show thee the best springs', II, 2, 164–76). In his next scene, he discovers his natural superiority to Trinculo; he instigates a perfectly coherent coup against Prospero; he displays a certain aesthetic sense in the 'Be not afeard; the isle is full of noises' speech (III, 2, 144–52), itself a leading instance of the islanders' capacity to see visions – and to suffer the breaking in of reality. Caliban's is the drive that sustains the plot, while the others succumb to the childish distractions of the garments. In this scene the realisation of Stephano's limitations, too, is beginning to dawn. Evidently it is Caliban's pattern to run through masters; he is a bad subject, though not in the usual sense. As the play continues, we discern the contours of a fully-capable being, one who voices self-knowledge ('He's but a sot, as I am', III, 2, 101), an appreciation of beauty (the praise of Miranda, III, 2, 106–10),[18] and a rudimentary moral sense, expressed in the ends-means equation of 'Do that good mischief' (IV, 1, 216). Wherever one touches the graph of Caliban's progress, the curve is up, until his final decision to seek for grace and acknowledge himself a fool. Technically, all this is expressed in the quality of his language. It is verse, itself a coded judgement that stamps Caliban as a being apart from Stephano and Trinculo. It moves from the club-footed stumping of

> As wicked dew as e'er my mother brush'd
> With raven's feather from unwholesome fen
> Drop on you both!
>
> (I, 2, 321–3)

to the rhythmic subtleties of 'Be not afeard' (III, 2, 144–52), and the free-moving, masculine energy of 'The dropsy drown this fool' (IV, 1, 230–4) and

> Ay, that I will; and I'll be wise hereafter
> And seek for grace. What a thrice-double ass
> Was I, to take this drunkard for a god
> And worship this dull fool!
>
> (V, 1, 294–7)

At the end, no guarantees for Caliban's future progress can be issued. Spiritually, the man is on probation. But his progress through this play composes a major statement of human potential: to be set against the explicit record of intended rape, murder, and a constitutional unwillingness to be governed by anyone but himself.

And he, Caliban, is the leading individual embodiment of what Gonzalo is talking about in his vision of collective man. Or rather, what Shakespeare is talking about; the presented object hereabouts (II, 1) is more complicated than the speech in itself appears to be. In context, the

'Commonwealth' speech occurs as a diversion for the grief-stricken Alonso and has, I think, the intention and force of a metaphysical poem.[16] It is not to be taken at face value. If one does – and no doubt this is often true of the play in performance – the speech becomes a kind of liberal editorial, assailed by heartless conservative correspondents who point out, correctly, that it will never work. This is effective enough on stage. To leave it there undervalues Gonzalo's intelligence and sophistication. He is surely setting up a slow-moving target, certain that Antonio and Sebastian cannot resist taking easy shots and thus create the diversion he wishes. Then, Sebastian and Antonio are incorporated into the passage in a sense of which they are entirely unaware. The thing will never work, *because* of Antonio and Sebastian. It is their presence, and not their criticisms, that invalidates the vision. And yet the vision has its own kind of truth, as so many from Sir Thomas More to William Morris have testified. The entire passage, which is in reality a single dialogue between Sebastian/Antonio and Gonzalo, creates a glowing awareness of human aspirations superimposed on human limitations. It is all reduced to a single exchange:

Miranda O brave new world,
That has such people in't!
Prospero 'Tis new to thee.
(v, 1, 184–5)

Prospero, be it noted, completes the line. Vision and reality would be incomplete without each other. Caliban, the New Commonwealth, the Miranda-Prospero exchange: all are variants of the same topic, man as he might be and man as he is.[17]

IV

Thus Caliban, jointly with Prospero, formulates the central problem of human governance. To attain his full potential, man must be free, which he is unfit to be; he must also exercise power, for which he is equally unfit. The first half of *The Tempest* expounds the necessity of wise government, the second its limitations. The dramatic disquisition enters its most difficult phase during the latter phase of the play. The action concerns the giving up of power, and its relations to love. Here it seems best to encounter openly a factor in contemporary perception. Almost inevitably, we see the latter stages of *The Tempest* in terms of decolonisation. It happens that the 1950s and 1960s have provided historical models of decolonisation on which to reflect; this, as a part-willed, part-orderly process on a large scale is new in the world's experience. And these events enter our consciousness as a massive analogue to *The Tempest*. It is always possible to argue that it is unhistorical, and wrong, to impose our contemporary consciousness on Shakespeare. I should prefer to say that we cannot do anything else. I think it perfectly arguable that Shakespeare divined certain psychic forces in man, a perception which as it happened preceded by three and a half centuries an actual historical demonstration of their reality. We have no difficulty in accepting *Julius Caesar* as a textbook analysis of dictatorship and its context, with a permanent relevance; why not accept *The Tempest* as containing a largely anticipatory account of political and psychological verities?

Viewed in this way, the events of *The Tempest* may lose something of the soft Romantic afterglow in which, critically speaking, they are still bathed. Here, for instance, is Philip Mason's response to the play:

> The settler mentality is not, then, created by the colonial situation. Shakespeare knew that it was there in human nature and drew the colonial type in Prospero, the escapist deeply reluctant to give up his magic, to leave his desert island and to return to the society of people who would argue with him. Prospero, you will remember, seldom speaks to Ariel, the good native, without reminding him of how grateful he ought to be because he was released from a cloven pine; Ariel reminds Prospero that he was promised self-government, and Prospero, who does not think he is ready for it, threatens to peg him inside the knotty entrails of an oak unless he will be obedient a little longer – but does not, as one might expect, offer him a knighthood if he would. Prospero usually bullies Miranda; to Caliban, the bad native, he is consistently harsh and justifies his harshness by Caliban's attempt to violate Miranda . . . Certainly Caliban provides a convincing picture of the mission boy who has not made good, of the degradation that results when the tribesman is prised away from his old background, transfers his dependence and then feels himself rejected.[18]

Partial as this sardonic account is, these categories from our modern consciousness fit the play with a disturbing ease. One could add, for instance, the problem of language. The much-discussed question of language as a form of cultural domination[19] parallels Caliban's rejection of his master's language:

> You taught me language; and my profit on 't
> Is, I know how to curse. The red plague rid you
> For learning me your language!
>
> (I, 2, 363–5)

History itself seems destined to act as dramatic criticism. In context, Mason is writing the foreword to Ottave Mannoni's classic study of the colonial mentality; and Mannoni chose Prospero and Caliban as metaphors for the relationships of dependence and mastery that are central in the colonial encounter. Hence the title of his work, *Prospero and Caliban: The Psychology of Colonization.* As it happens, the particular analysis of *The Tempest* that Mannoni supplies[20] is rather unsatisfactory, since it presses too hard upon the adverse features of Prospero's mind and urges a motive of repressed sexual guilt, where few will be able to follow him. The merit of M. Mannoni's exposition – to literary critics, that is – lies rather in its main drift, that a distinguished anthropologist and psychologist finds in *The Tempest* a mirror for the colonial experience. It is clear to him that 'Shakespeare's theme is the drama of renunciation of power and domination, which are symbolised by magic, a borrowed power which must be rendered up. Man must learn to accept himself as he is and to accept others as they are, even if they happen to be called Caliban.'[21] Prospero's power is a technological skill, that is to say an essentially temporary manifestation of superiority. For a time it affords domination over the archetypes of the Good Native and the Bad Native, both of whom, interestingly, display the characteristic of ingratitude.[22] Caliban goes further: 'They all do hate him / As rootedly as I' (III, 2, 102–3). Power, absolute and externally imposed, is not loved. In the civilised consciousness, the problem of authority is ultimately that of securing love. The play suggests the paradox that while love is power, love is to be gained through the renunciation of power.

At bottom the exercise of power is inseparable from the problem of giving up power. The awareness of this is embryonically present in Shakespeare so early as *Henry VI*. The matter is given full exposition in *Richard II* and *King Lear*, and *The Tempest* presents Shakespeare's definitive treatment. What is unique here is that Prospero gives up power prematurely. He is not compelled by force majeure, since he dominates political opposition, nor by the immediate pressures of age, since he is in a vigorous late maturity. The decision is taken on unspecified grounds: it is the business of the play, and not a soliloquy, to offer an explanation. The events themselves define the meaning of the act.

V

The recessional, the slow movement away from power begins in Act IV. It follows hard upon the exultant cries of triumphant authority. 'My high charms work . . . They now are in my pow'r (III, 3, 88–90). Never has Ariel been so submissive: 'What would my potent master? Here I am' (IV, 1, 34). Prospero wills a masque, a Durbar in theatre. But now he speaks of 'your last service' – 'last' is 'recent' here, but the word has a ring – then, disturbingly, 'Some vanity of mine art' (IV, 1, 35, 41). 'Vanity' means 'show', but the undertone of worldly emptiness and futility are there. And now Ariel asks a strange question : 'Do you love me, master? no?' (IV, 1, 48) The unexpected fifth line of the song is almost coquettish : the implied impulse is of curiosity, not care. The feeling is all in Prospero's answer, 'Dearly, my delicate Ariel', and it is his first admission that he loves Ariel. The masque is Prospero's scenario of the future :

> Spirits, which by mine art
> I have from their confines call'd to enact
> My present fancies.
>
> (IV, 1, 120–2)

His imagination projects the failure of Cupid to anticipate the 'bed-right', hence the vision parallels the admonition he has twice previously urged on Ferdinand. It is fantasy and homily in combination. But it is not a prediction. Prospero can order matters immediate : 'No tongue! all eyes! be silent.' (IV, 1, 59) He cannot will the future, he can only try to influence its course by advice, entreaty, and a vision of its splendours. The limits of power are now, in broad contour, indicated.

Following the irruption of the conspirators upon this vision, Prospero delivers the great 'Our revels now are ended' speech. It proposes the stage as a metaphor for temporal majesty, and for mortality itself. The transition from vehicle to tenor is mediated by our awareness that the towers, clouds, etc., may well be literal stage props :

> These our actors,
> As I foretold you, were all spirits and
> Are melted into air, into thin air;
> And, like the baseless fabric of this vision,
> The cloud-capp'd tow'rs, the gorgeous palaces,
> The solemn temples, the great globe itself,
> Yea, all which it inherit, shall dissolve
> And, like this insubstantial pageant faded,
> Leave not a rack behind.
>
> (IV, 1, 148–58)

This passage is hard to read precisely. Is 'actors' the continuing subject of 'are melted', 'shall dissolve', 'Leave not a rack behind'? If not, what is the subject of 'dissolve'? As one first reads the passage, one's mind accepts 'The cloud-capp'd tow'rs . . . the great globe itself' as in apposition to 'the baseless fabric'. If one holds on to this sense of the construction, then 'actors' survives, mentally, as the subject of 'dissolves'. Yet the magnetic power of 'dissolve' draws to itself 'globe' as the felt subject. In that case we have, retrospectively, to shift our sense of the syntax, for 'cloud-capp'd tow'rs' is now a comparison with 'baseless fabric' – and is, therefore, real. 'Like' (line 151) can look backwards to 'actor', or forward to 'tow'rs'. The plurality of subjects, in addition to two 'likes', make it impossible to pin down a single grammatical sense.[28] The ambivalences of the speech – which stem from the initial, semantic ambiguity of 'actor' – convey with a total exactitude its force, which is to blur the category-distinction between mortality and stage – and between tenor and vehicle. The piercing immediacy of the conclusion is normally somewhat lost in performance. Actors will customarily read 'We are such stuff /As *dreams* are made on . . .' which is to poeticise, not to say romanticise the phrase. The true movement of the speech accents the phrase's first word as the emerging reality: '*We* are such stuff / As dreams are made on . . .' and the pain of the intimation is apparent.

The movement away from power gathers momentum as the promises to grant freedom thicken. Prospero broods over his failure with Caliban (IV, 1, 188–92), another representative of the matters over which he has no control. He defines then the formal objective of his action:

> they being penitent
> The sole drift of my purpose doth extend
> Not a frown further.
>
> (V, 1, 28–30)

And immediately afterwards, his invocation to 'Ye elves of hills', an imperial proclamation of the triumphs of his 'so potent art', ends

> But this rough magic
> I here abjure, and, when I have requir'd
> Some heavenly music, which even now I do,
> To work mine end upon their senses that
> This airy charm is for, I'll break my staff,
> Bury it certain fathoms in the earth,
> And deeper than did ever plummet sound
> I'll drown my book.
>
> *Solemn music*
>
> (V, 1, 50–7)

The 'solemn music' intimates the harmonies of the conclusion. The recessional is modulating into a nunc dimittis. But it is important to note that Prospero does not give up all authority, simply his 'art'. The final intent to 'retire me to my Milan' does not, of course, correspond to 'retirement' in our modern sense, and the implication is that Prospero intends to govern Milan by normal methods.[24]

The final exercise of Prospero's authority is to make those under him perceive, so far as they can, the truth. Reason, knowledge, grace are the words to which the action now relates itself. 'Their understanding / Begins to swell, and the approaching tide / Will shortly fill the reasonable shore' says Prospero (v, 1, 79–81). '. . . all of us found ourselves / When no man was his own' is Gonzalo's summary of the Prosperous Voyage (v, 1, 212–13). 'Some oracle / Must rectify our knowledge' says Alonso (v, 1, 244–5). Caliban's decision to seek for grace, coupled with his rejection of the false god Stephano, is itself an act of self-awareness. Revelation, as in a 'dream' (v, 1, 239), if not understanding, is the lot of the Boatswain. The silences of Antonio and Sebastian constitute the major reservations to the movement. Self-knowledge is the state to which the islanders aspire. It is all focused to Prospero, for whom the giving up of power is a personal, as it is in a wider context, route to self-knowledge. It is approached through an acknowledgement of responsibility ('this thing of darkness I / Acknowledge mine'), of territorial and political possession('my Milan'), and of relationship ('My Ariel'). This last sad paradox – what can '*my* Ariel' mean? – is the reduction of the relationships that define self. *The Tempest* is what Prospero has learnt: the total play becomes the expression of the civilised consciousness. And that consciousness reveals itself, above all, in the last few lines:

> My Ariel, chick,
> That is thy charge: then to the elements
> Be free, and fare thou well! Please you, draw near.

A final expression of love, a granting of freedom, a request to others to draw near: it is the conclusive statement of a play that has begun with an order, and ends with a request.

The Epilogue renders all down to an abdication that substitutes prayer for power. There is undeniably a suggestion that Prospero's 'art to enchant' is a metaphor for the power of the dramatist; it is an allusion whose attraction many have felt, but it remains unpursuable. For the rest, the Epilogue is a coda that restates and enlarges the meaning of the play's final lines. If we blank out all but the pronouns, it reads:

... my ....
.... I ... mine own
....
I .... you
.... me ....
... I ... my ....
....
.... your ......
.... me ...... my ....
.... your ....
.... yours ....
.... my ....
.... I ....
....
... my ....
...... I ....
....
....
... you ....
... your .... me ...

Stripped of inessentials, the message is even clearer. The broken insistences of *I*, *my*, *your*, *you* convey the true theme. We call some of these pronouns *possessive*, and the category reminds us of the ultimate precipitation of power in *The Tempest* : *my*, *your*. Imagery dies into syntax. The resolution of the play becomes a surrender of the self into the power of others. The rhythm of *The Tempest*, whatever the actor's delivery, compels the reading of the final words 'set *me* free'. It foreshadows that state to which Prospero looks forward, and for which 'freedom' itself may be a metaphor.

Notes

References are to *The Complete Works of Shakespeare*, edited by Hardin Craig and David Bevington (Glenview, Ill., 1973). Statistics of word-frequencies are taken from Marvin Spevack, *A Complete and Systematic Concordance to the Works of Shakespeare*, 6 vols. (Hildesheim, 1968–70).

INTRODUCTION

1. *The Daily Telegraph*, 25 Jan. 1965, p. 1.
2. See especially Patricia Thomson, 'Rant and Cant in *Troilus and Cressida*,' *Essays and Studies* edited for the English Association by Francis Berry (London, 1969).
3. A. D. Nuttall, *Two Concepts of Allegory* (London, 1967) p. 21.
4. For an illustration, see E. H. Gombrich, *Art and Illusion* (London, 1960), p. 5.
5. This is argued in detail in my *Shakespeare's Comedies: Explorations in Form* (Princeton, 1972) pp. 113–45.

CHAPTER 1: RICHARD III: PLAYER AND KING

1. A. P. Rossiter, *Angel With Horns* (London, 1961) p. 2.
2. Nicholas Brooke, *Shakespeare's Early Tragedies* (London, 1968) p. 56.
3. Laurence Olivier's delivery of this soliloquy directly into the camera (in his film of *Richard III*) made the audience an accomplice, a kind of collective Catesby.
4. For a review of the rhetoric hereabouts, together with the interpretative possibilities, see Wolfgang Clemen, *A Commentary on Shakespeare's Richard III* (London, 1968) pp. 3–4.
5. Susan Sontag, 'Notes on Camp', in *Against Interpretation* (New York, 1966) p. 277.
6. Ibid., p. 286.
7. Ibid., p. 280.
8. M. C. Bradbrook, *The Rise of the Common Player* (London, 1962) pp. 133–5.
9. Sontag (New York, 1966) p. 280. Clemen remarks that 'Richard's peculiar speech seems to be the first example of Shakespeare's characterising a

person through language.' Wolfgang Clemen, 'Tradition and Originality in Shakespeare's *Richard III*', *Shakespeare Quarterly*, v (1954) 255.

10. John Palmer, *Political Characters of Shakespeare* (London, 1945) p. 88.
11. Sontag (New York, 1966) p. 287.
12. Perhaps 'rejected' would be more appropriate than 'unwanted', since Richard himself excludes 'the lascivious pleasings of a lute. / But I . . .' (I, 1, 13–14)
13. Johan Huizinga, *Homo Ludens* (Boston, 1955) p. 40.
14. And, curiously, the lives of the acting profession as we know it. As is well known, a first-class actor will often speak of the challenge, the risk of performing before a live audience.
15. Huizinga (Boston, 1955) p. 39.
16. Emrys Jones, *Scenic Form in Shakespeare* (Oxford, 1971) p. 74.
17. 'Richard himself appears in a dazzling series of roles, all of which are completely successful. Through five long acts, he manages to deceive virtually everyone around him . . .' Anne Righter, *Shakespeare and the Idea of the Play* (London, 1962) p. 97. I think it truer to say that he deceives hardly anyone. But people do misjudge him.
18. 'Conscience avant *Richard*'s himself again' is the line in Colley Cibber's version of *Richard III*. It is Act v, scene v, line 85 in Christopher S. Spencer's *Five Restoration Adaptations of Shakespeare* (Urbana, Ill., 1965).
19. *OED*, sense 6b.

CHAPTER 2: KING JOHN: SOME BASTARDS TOO

1. E. M. W. Tillyard, *Shakespeare's History Plays* (New York, 1962) p. 21.
2. Irving Ribner, *The English History Play in the Age of Shakespeare* (London, 1965) pp. 124–5.
3. Sigurd Burckhardt, *Shakespearean Meanings* (Princeton, 1968) p. 138.
4. John F. Danby identifies the 'new thought' in *King John*, 'that the unity and integrity of England is the overriding moral claim.' *Shakespeare's Doctrine of Nature* (London, 1948) p. 79.
5. E. A. J. Honigmann (ed.), *King John*, New Arden edition (London, 1959) p. lx.
6. This is well argued by Adrien Bonjour in 'The Road to Swinstead Abbey', *ELH*, XVIII (1951) 253–74.
7. Tillyard has voiced a common complaint: 'Shakespeare huddles together and fails to motivate properly the events of the last third of his play.' Tillyard (New York, 1962) p. 215. Similarly with Robert Ornstein, for whom the last scenes are a 'muddle'. *A Kingdom for a Stage* (Cambridge, Mass., 1972) p. 84. This is true: but surely the dramatist's intention is to strengthen the impression of perplexity and accelerating decline.
8. The significance of the Bastard's kneeling to Henry is fully analysed in James L. Calderwood, 'Commodity and Honour in *King John*', *University of Toronto Quarterly*, XXIX (1960) 341–56, and William H. Matchett, 'Richard's Divided Heritage in *King John*', *Essays in Criticism*, XII (1962)

231–53. His conclusion, that 'the play has demonstrated the moral complexity of the problem of loyalty', is particularly apposite to my argument here.

CHAPTER 3: ROMEO AND JULIET: THE SONNET-WORLD OF VERONA

1. Susan Snyder argues that 'the reversal is so radical as to constitute a change of genre.' '*Romeo and Juliet*: Comedy into Tragedy', *Essays in Criticism*, XX (1970) 391. This leads to her final verdict that 'what Shakespeare wanted to convey was an ironic dissociation between character and the direction of events,' and that 'although the central characters have their weaknesses, their destruction does not really stem from these weaknesses.' (401). This analysis rests, I suggest, on a reaction to the play's mood, which unquestionably shifts from comedy to tragedy. My argument here is that the play, contrary to the impression one receives in the audience, does actually move in an (intellectually) straight line: that is, the catastrophe stems from certain communal and individual weaknesses that are correctly diagnosed from the beginning.
2. Wolfgang Clemen, *The Development of Shakespeare's Imagery* (London, 1951) p. 64.
3. Harry Levin well emphasises the bookishness of Veronese society in 'Form and Formality in *Romeo and Juliet*', *Shakespeare Quarterly*, XI (1960) 4–5.
4. *Delia*, Sonnet XL: and *Diana*, Sonnet VI in the manuscript edition. The quotations are from the joint volume in the *Elizabethan Sonnet Cycles* series, edited by Martha Foote Crow (London, 1896).
5. Patrick Cruttwell, *The Shakespearean Moment* (New York, 1960) p. 18. Cruttwell's main argument, concerning the decisive transitional conflicts of the 1590's, is both persuasive in itself and parallel to my own reading of *Romeo and Juliet*.
6. J. W. Lever, *The Elizabethan Love Sonnet*, second edn. (London, 1966) p. 146.
7. Ibid., p. 57.
8. 'It develops and broadens – vulgarises, if you will – the irony of the bridal music brought to the deathbed.' Harley Granville-Barker, *Prefaces to Shakespeare*, 2 vols. (London, 1958) II, p. 319.
9. Cruttwell has a perceptive commentary on this sonnet and its relations with the convention. Cruttwell (New York, 1960) pp. 18–19.
10. See Brian Vickers, *The Artistry of Shakespeare's Prose* (London, 1968) p. 73.
11. A. J. Smith, 'The Poetry of John Donne', in *English Poetry and Prose 1540–1674*, ed. Christopher Ricks (London, 1970) p. 148.
12. The fourteen sonnets in which 'name' appears are 36, 39, 71, 72, 76, 80, 81, 89, 95, 108, 111, 127, 136, 151.
13. R. M. Frye, *Shakespeare and Christian Doctrine* (Princeton, 1963) pp. 24–7.
14. F. M. Dickey, *Not Wisely But Too Well* (San Marino, Calif., 1957).

15. In his Commentary to the Laurel edition of *Romeo and Juliet* (New York, 1958).
16. It is true that the reconciliation of Montague and Capulet can itself be a theatrical statement of knowledge. Once only have I seen this affectingly played: by the RSC (1976). After the Prince's penultimate speech, a long pause elapsed before Capulet hesitantly extended his hand, with 'O brother Montague, give me thy hand'.
17. Robert O. Evans, *The Osier Cage: Rhetorical Devices in Romeo and Juliet* (Lexington, Kentucky, 1966) p. 82.

CHAPTER 4: HENRY V: THE REASON WHY

1. So reputable a production as Michael Benthall's at the Old Vic (Dec. 1955) cut the first scene in its entirety.
2. For example, Gerald Gould, 'A New Reading of *Henry V*', *The English Review* (1919); John Palmer, *Political Characters of Shakespeare* (London 1945) pp. 180–249; Harold C. Goddard, *The Meaning of Shakespeare*, 2 vols. (Chicago, 1951) I, pp. 215–68; Roy W. Battenhouse, '*Henry V* as Heroic Comedy', in *Essays on Shakespeare and Elizabethan Drama*, ed. Richard Hosley (Columbia, Missouri, 1962) pp. 163–82.
3. Trevor Nunn, in an interview with the author. See Ralph Berry, *On Directing Shakespeare: Interviews with Contemporary Directors* (London and New York, 1977), p. 58.
4. Next comes *The Merchant of Venice*, with thirty-one occurrences; then *3 Henry VI*, with thirty; *2 Henry VI*, twenty-eight; *Love's Labour's Lost*, twenty-six.
5. Robert Hapgood, 'Shakespeare's Thematic Modes of Speech: *Richard II* to *Henry V*', *Shakespeare Survey 20* (1967) 41–9.
6. L. C. Knights, *Public Voices* (London, 1971) p. 36.
7. C. H. Hobday, 'Imagery and Irony in *Henry V*', *Shakespeare Survey 21* (1968), 110–11, following Goddard (Chicago, 1951) pp. 220–2.
8. The Scriptural authority caps the argument; but an argument resting on such remote authorities is evidently less than convincing. Sister Miriam Joseph classifies the passage as apomnemonysis: 'The figure apomnemonysis is a form of inartificial argument which quotes for authority the testimony of approved authors', *Shakespeare's Use of the Arts of Language* (New York, 1947) p. 102. As she points out, the habit of quoting from texts was matter for satire in *Love's Labour's Lost*, and Holofernes' 'And certes the text most infallibly concludes it' (IV, 2, 170) offers a nice parallel to the Archbishop's mode of reasoning. The technique of arguing from Macedon to Monmouth is of course fully exposed elsewhere in *Henry V*, and Richard Levin has recently supplied a devastating analysis of the shortcomings of that method. See 'On Fluellen's Figures, Christ Figures, and James Figures', *PMLA*, LXXXIX (1974) 302–11.
9. Thomas Wilson, *The Arte of Rhetorique*, ed. G. H. Mair (Oxford, 1909) p. 197; quoted by Sister Miriam Joseph (New York, 1947) p. 327.

10. Alvin Kernan, 'The Henriad: Shakespeare's Major History Plays', in *Modern Shakespearean Criticism*, ed. Kernan (New York, 1970) p. 273.
11. As an illustration of the Elizabethan sense of the distinction, consider Walsingham's 'I call God to witness, that as a private person I have done nothing unbeseeming an honest man, nor, as I bear the place of a public man, have I done anything unworthy of my place.' Conyers Read, *Mr Secretary Walsingham and the Policy of Queen Elizabeth*, 3 vols. (Oxford, 1925) III, p. 53.
12. See Palmer (London, 1945) pp. 238–40; Goddard (Chicago, 1951) pp. 242–4.
13. Goddard (Chicago, 1951) p. 242.
14. Palmer (London, 1945) p. 238.
15. Ibid., p. 242.
16. The soliloquy is curiously public, generalised. It may be worth recalling that Colley Cibber purloined a portion of it for his *Richard III* – and assigned it to Lady Anne.
17. Winston S. Churchill, *A History of the English-Speaking Peoples*, vol. 1 (London, 1956) pp. 315–16.

CHAPTER 5: 'TO SAY ONE': AN ESSAY ON HAMLET

1. John Dover Wilson, *What Happens in Hamlet* (Cambridge, 1935) p. 272. Dover Wilson's suggestion on 'one' is now retained in *The Riverside Shakespeare*, ed. G. Blakemore Evans *et al.* (Boston, 1974).
2. L. C. Knights, *Some Shakespearean Themes and An Approach to Hamlet* (Stanford, 1966) p. 191 *et seq.*
3. Harry Levin, *The Question of Hamlet* (New York, 1961) p. 69.
4. The complement to Hamlet here is, as so often, Claudius. We have only one opportunity to observe his mind at close quarters, but he uses it to think hard – and accurately – about the issues. 'May one be pardoned and retain the offence?' (III, 3, 56) is a brutally precise way of stating the problem.
5. David Horowitz, *Shakespeare: An Existentialist View* (London, 1965) p. 39.
6. Maynard Mack, 'The World of *Hamlet*', *Yale Review*, XLI (1952) 513.
7. Michael Goldman, *Shakespeare and the Energies of Drama* (Princeton, 1972) pp. 74–93.
8. Ibid., p. 74.
9. See especially Maurice Charney, *Style in Hamlet* (Princeton, 1969) pp. 6–30; Nigel Alexander, *Poison, Play and Duel* (London, 1971); Kenneth Muir, *Shakespeare the Professional* (London, 1973) pp. 123–6.
10. M. M. Mahood, *Shakespeare's Wordplay* (London, 1957) pp. 116–17.

CHAPTER 6: TROILUS AND CRESSIDA: TEMPUS EDAX RERUM

1. See B. Ifor Evans, *The Language of Shakespeare's Plays* (London, 1964) pp. 141–2.

2. Patricia Thomson analyses very convincingly the stylistic implications of *Troilus and Cressida*, especially of its 'high-swelling' and 'affected' language. 'Rant and cant, throughout Shakespeare's career and whatever his audience, serve the purposes of his comedy and satire.' 'Rant and cant in *Troilus and Cressida*', *Essays and Studies* edited for the English Association by Francis Berry (London, 1969) p. 36.
3. For a close analysis of their interdependence, see Richard Levin, *The Multiple Plot in the English Renaissance Drama* (Chicago, 1971) pp. 160–8.
4. This is not to acquiesce in Ulysses' 'daughter of the game' charge; it is curious that so many critics treat the comment as Holy Writ. The context is clear enough, a certain antagonism between Ulysses and Cressida that surfaces in Cressida's 'Why, beg, then' and Ulysses' rejection of her (IV, 5, 47–52). After which Ulysses gets his retaliation in first. His version is the one that goes on the record.

   The rehabilitation of Cressida marks a groundswell of modern criticism. The best and most sympathetic treatment of her that I know is Joseph Papp's, developed with masterly insight in his essay 'Directing *Troilus and Cressida*' in *The Festival Shakespeare Troilus and Cressida* (New York, 1967) pp. 23–72.
5. For instance, by Una Ellis-Fermor, in 'The Universe of *Troilus and Cressida*', *The Frontiers of Drama* (London, 1964) pp. 60–1. I prefer Robert Kimbrough's assessment: 'All is rant so far – but rant majestically phrased', *Shakespeare's Troilus and Cressida and its Setting* (Cambridge, Mass., 1964) p. 138. The matter is debated thoroughly by T. McAlindon and Mark Sacharoff, the former stressing the hollow and unconstructive nature of Agamemnon's address, the latter its eloquence and decorum. 'Critical Comment in Response to T. McAlindon's "Language, Style, and Meaning in *Troilus and Cressida*"', *PMLA*, LXXXVII (1972) 90–9. We need the play to read the address, but its immediate deficiency is one of content.
6. 'Fame' is the theme of Navarre's opening speech, an ambition which the play (and the Princess, IV, 1, 30–5) refutes.
7. See Caroline Spurgeon's table in *Shakespeare's Imagery* (Cambridge, 1935) Chart VII, and her account of the play's images, pp. 321–4.
8. A useful commentary on the disease and animal images is in Brian Vickers, *The Artistry of Shakespeare's Prose* (London, 1968) pp. 276–94.
9. See especially Mark Rose, *Shakespearean Design* (Cambridge, Mass., 1972).
10. David Horowitz, *Shakespeare: An Existentialist View* (London, 1965) p. 103.
11. For a commentary on the explicit Time-references, see G. Wilson Knight, *The Wheel of Fire* (London, 1930) pp. 65–9.
12. Erwin Panofsky, *Studies in Iconology: Humanistic Themes in the Art of the Renaissance* (New York, 1962) p. 74.
13. Ibid., p. 83. See also F. Saxl, 'Veritas Filia Temporis', in *Philosophy and History: Essays Presented to Ernst Cassirer* (Oxford, 1936) pp. 197–222.

14. Samuel C. Chew, *The Virtues Reconciled: An Iconographic Study* (Toronto, 1947) p. 90.
15. Of an earlier statement by Troilus to the same effect (II, 2, 61–5), L. C. Knights comments: 'Yet what could be more absurd than to speak of the senses as mediating between the judgment and the will? It is the judgment that is the pilot or mediator between the senses and the will.' *Some Shakespearean Themes and An Approach to Hamlet* (Stanford, 1966) p. 75.
16. For a reading of the play's three endings that differs significantly from the following, see R. A. Foakes, *Shakespeare: The Dark Comedies to the Last Plays: From Satire to Celebration* (London, 1971) pp. 58–60.
17. Vickers (London, 1968) p. 294.
18. Geoffrey Bullough (ed.), *The Narrative and Dramatic Sources of Shakespeare* (London, 1966) vol. 6.
19. Quotations are taken from *Shakespeare's Ovid: Being Arthur Golding's Translation of the Metamorphoses*, ed. W. H. D. Rouse (London, 1904).

CHAPTER 7: SEXUAL IMAGERY IN CORIOLANUS

1. Maurice Morgann, 'An Essay on the Dramatic Character of Sir John Falstaff', reprinted in Maurice Morgann, *Shakespearian Criticism*, ed. Daniel A. Fineman (Oxford, 1972) p. 149.
2. D. B. Wyndham Lewis, *The Lion and the Fox* (London, 1951) p. 244. The same view of the play is taken by I. R. Browning in 'Coriolanus: Boy of Tears', *Essays in Criticism*, v (1955) 18–31. There is an excellent analysis of the Volumnia–Coriolanus relationship in Harold C. Goddard (Chicago, 1951) II, pp. 212–25.

   Coriolanus is strongly oedipal in its configurations, and one would expect the psychoanalytic commentators to throw some light on it. Freud, curiously, did not write on the play, though Shakespeare was one of his favourite authors. But as Norman N. Holland's useful survey of psychoanalytic criticism shows, there is a fair degree of consensus. Several writers

   > see Coriolanus' personality developmentally, as growing out of his relation to his mother, in particular, her frustration of his needs in early infancy to be dependent. Recent psychoanalytic data about the first months of life say this kind of early oral frustration would lead to a permanent build-up of aggressive energy . . .; it would lead to an inability to tolerate being dependent and to a blurred differentiation of self from love object (Coriolanus' need to prove himself, win an identity, through achievement, countered by his tendency to identify with his mother).

   Norman N. Holland, *Psychoanalysis and Shakespeare* (New York, 1966) p. 161. David B. Barron, in a striking article, discerns a connection between Coriolanus' infancy and his attitude to the Roman famine. '*Coriolanus*: Portrait of the Artist as Infant', *The American Imago*, xix (1962) 171–93. 'We can infer that under his mother's influence Coriolanus learned to discipline his hunger' (174); he hates the Roman crowd, who can't. For Barron, the weaning process is 'conceived as a physical trauma, and the transition from mother's breast to battlefield suggests the displacement of his feeding, onto other external objects. It is as if the mother, then, had diverted her son's appetites from herself to his enemies . . .' (173). This type of speculation appears more proper to *Coriolanus* than any other play in the canon. The relationship of mother to son is not a mere technical recess, but an area of the play's imaginative hinterland that we are surely invited to reflect upon. And at all times we have to remember that the strict category-division between politics and psychology is ours – not Shakespeare's.

3. See T. J. B. Spencer (ed.), *Shakespeare's Plutarch* (Harmondsworth, 1964) p. 300.
4. Una Ellis-Fermor, '*Coriolanus*', *Shakespeare the Dramatist* (London, 1961) pp. 60–77.
5. *Coriolanus*, ed. Harry Levin, Pelican edn. (Baltimore, 1956) p. 20.
6. A. P. Rossiter, *Angel With Horns* (London, 1961) p. 247.
7. Maurice Charney, *Shakespeare's Roman Plays* (Cambridge, Mass., 1961) p. 35.
8. G. Wilson Knight, 'The Royal Occupation: An Essay on *Coriolanus*', *The Imperial Theme* (London, 1951) p. 197.
9. An opportunity fully taken in, for example, Sir Tyrone Guthrie's production of *Coriolanus* at the Nottingham Playhouse, 1963.
10. Thomas Hobbes, *Leviathan*, Chapter xi.

CHAPTER 8: THE TEMPEST

1. Edward Dowden, *Shakespere: His Mind and Art* (London, 1875) p. 423; quoted by A. D. Nuttall in *Two Concepts of Allegory* (London, 1967) p. 1.
2. Nuttall (London, 1967) p. 160.
3. Caroline Spurgeon, *Shakespeare's Imagery* (Cambridge, 1935) pp. 300–4.
4. Reuben A. Brower, *The Fields of Light: An Experiment in Critical Reading* (New York, 1951) p. 97.
5. Ibid., p. 120.
6. Ibid., p. 121.
7. Witold Ostrowski, 'A Forgotten Meaning of *The Tempest*', in *Poland's Homage to Shakespeare*, ed. S. Helsztynski (Warsaw, 1965) p. 166.
8. Frank Kermode, in the Introduction to his New Arden edition of *The Tempest* (London, 1954) p. xlvii.
9. 'Prospero finds his reasons not in the divine analogy he shadows forth, but in his participation in mankind.' Thomas McFarland, *Shakespeare's Pastoral Comedy* (Chapel Hill, North Carolina, 1972) p. 171.
10. The uppermost associations are clearly of courtly love. See Kermode's note to the passage: (London, 1954) pp. 122–3.
11. One is reminded here of John Holloway's comment on *King Lear*: 'love

(unless that word is taken, as I fear it is often taken, to mean every good thing) is a value with a great but finite place in human life.' *The Story of the Night* (London, 1961) p. 91. The game of chess implies a situation in which love will not be enough.

12. See generally Mark Rose, *Shakespearean Design* (Cambridge, Mass) 1972.
13. G. Wilson Knight, *The Shakespearian Tempest* (London, 1968) p. 258.
14. 'His physical deformity is index of his moral status.' Howard Felperin, *Shakespearean Romance* (Princeton, 1972) p. 263. The opposite approach is more usually found in stage productions.
15. This is the more creditable to Caliban if we follow most modern editors (and stage directors, to my observation) in assigning the scolding of I, 2, 352–62 to Miranda.
16. I agree with Joan Hartwig that 'Gonzalo's tone is whimsical'. *Shakespeare's Tragi-comic Vision* (Baton Rouge, Louisiana, 1972) p. 148.
17. Naturally, this idea is realised dramatically through other means: for instance, the termination of the banquet by the news of the conspiracy.
18. Philip Mason, in his Foreword to Ottave Mannoni's *Prospero and Caliban: The Psychology of Colonization* (New York, 1964) p. 12.
19. See, for example, Frantz Fanon's discussion of the topic in 'The Negro and Language', *Black Skin, White Masks* (New York, 1967) pp. 17–40.
20. Mannoni (New York, 1964) pp. 105–9.
21. Ibid., p. 105.
22. Mason cites the colonial commonplace, 'the natives are never grateful', ibid., p. 9.
23. This is reminiscent of the difficulties that Stephen Booth detects in identifying a syntactical pattern in the Sonnets. See especially his chapter on 'False Starts and Changes of Direction' in *An Essay on Shakespeare's Sonnets* (New Haven, 1969) pp. 51–60.
24. D. G. James sees Prospero as returning to his real work. *The Dream of Prospero* (Oxford, 1967) p. 126.

Index